The Texas Governor

by June Rayfield Welch

Dallas ● Yellow Rose Press ● 1977

Library of Congress Catalog Card No.
77-93050

ISBN 0-912854-09-X

First Printing December 1977
Second Edition September 1986

Published by
Yellow Rose Press
Dallas, Texas

Printed by

Waco, Texas

For Jenny and Frank Hall
Who remembered, and tried to tell me.

The Author

June Rayfield Welch has degrees from Texas Christian University, the University of Texas at Arlington, Texas Tech University and George Washington University. He practiced law prior to becoming Academic Dean of the University of Dallas, where he is presently chairman of the Department of History. He served in the Merchant Marine, was a sergeant in the Army, and is now an Air Force Reserve lieutenant colonel. His books include: A FAMILY HISTORY; THE TEXAS COURTHOUSE; TEXAS: NEW PERSPECTIVES; HISTORIC SITES OF TEXAS; DAVE'S TUNE, a novel; PEOPLE AND PLACES IN THE TEXAS PAST; THE GLORY THAT WAS TEXAS; AND HERE'S TO CHARLEY BOYD, a novel; and GOING GREAT IN THE LONE STAR STATE.

Introduction

Most years in Gainesville we gave very little thought to the governors of Texas, perhaps because we were only ten miles from Oklahoma. ("Alfalfa Bill" Murray, formerly of Collinsville, had been governor there and was still a presence.) But that changed in the middle thirties; everyone in nearby Wichita Falls ran for governor, and young Jimmy Allred won the right to host the celebration of the hundredth anniversary of Texas independence. (Dallas had the main event in 1936, but Fort Worth imported Billy Rose and Paul Whiteman's band and advertised "Dallas for culture, Fort Worth for fun.")

The Texas Centennial year was an exciting time. Visitors came from all over the world to the big birthday party. The 3¢ stamp on first class mail was an engraving of the Alamo inset with portraits of Travis and Bowie. Many great new buildings were opened at Dallas' Fair Park for the Centennial. College boys, earning tuition dollars and getting in shape for the football season, trotted over the grounds pulling rickshaws bearing tired visitors; Texans stood in long lines to be awed by such marvels as television and the midget village.

Everywhere there was music—great orchestras from Mexico, phonograph records played over primitive public address systems, college marching bands, steam calliopes, and religious quartets. In particular, there were yodeling brakemen and cowboys who sang mainly through the nose. (Leonard Slye, there as one of the Sons of the Pioneers, attracted some attention, changed his name to Roy Rogers and married Dale Evans, of Uvalde.) Gene Autry came to Dallas to make a singing-cowboy movie with a Centennial setting.

The radio had stimulated demand for music of all kinds. In North Texas tastes ran to country and western (or hillbilly, as it was then called) much to the chagrin of lovers of popular, and serious, music. The Grand Old Opry and the National Barn Dance came from far away and commanded huge listening audiences. In Texas no single person or group had more to do with the popularity of that kind of music than the Light Crust Doughboys. Walking home from school at noon on a warm day one could hear the entire program through the open windows. The announcer, W. Lee O'Daniel, attracted a huge following. After he acquired his own company, O'Daniel used his band to sell Hillbilly Flour.

When, in 1938, O'Daniel set out to become the leader of the people, Texas politics underwent a sudden and vigorous transformation. For the first time a candidate boasted of his lack of knowledge of politics and made no secret of his failure ever to vote in a Texas election. O'Daniel indicted "professional politicians" for unspecified wrongs and promised pensions to the old folks. With his Hillbilly Boys band and songs and poems celebrating home and mother, O'Daniel generated as much excitement along the Red River as he did in Austin-on-the-Colorado. As his campaign song, the candidate used his own composition, "My Million Dollar Smile." Seldom heard in recent years—or even then—the first verse went:

Come listen, folks, to what I say,
I've said goodbye to "gloomy day;"
I've got myself back on the track
And from here on I'm coming back;
Sob stuff for me is now taboo,
I've joined America's smiling crew;

I've tossed my troubles in the old trash pile,
And I'm wearing My Million Dollar Smile.

My father would snort and sneer at O'Daniel's inexperience and disinterest in acquiring an understanding of state government, and my aunt would simply rule any such arguments immaterial by a reminder that the Fort Worth flour salesman "was a fine Christian gentleman."

Governors since O'Daniel have been less colorful but longer on performance. On the whole Texans have used good judgment in choosing their first magistrates. When there was war with Mexico, Governor Henderson led Texas troops into battle. As secession loomed, "Old Sam Jacinto" warned Texans of the consequences of disunion; then Frank Lubbock tried to fulfill the state's obligations to the Confederacy. Jim Hogg thwarted the railroads' attempts to control Texas, and the Fergusons fought the Ku Klux Klan. It is hard to imagine better men than George Wood and Sul Ross and Oran Roberts and Pat Neff. This book is a brief introduction to the governors of Texas; they are worthy of our interest.

I am beholden to Chris La Plante and Jean Carefoot of the Texas Archives and the very able staff at the Austin Public Library who work with the Austin-Travis County Collection. Raff Frano continues making my photographs look better than they are. Nick and Joan Curtis designed this dandy dust jacket; Lynn Guier drew the map showing the old limits of the Republic. Once more Clark Coursey let me use his maps to show the origins of the governors. (Much investigation failed to reveal Peter Bell's hometown. As a Ranger he must have spent his entire time prior to election at various camps in South Texas or on the frontier. I used the Travis County map because his sojourn as governor was apparently the only time he came to rest anywhere in Texas.) Sister Ruth Quatman obtained materials and kept me posted on library due dates. Sister Frances Marie Manning checked the manuscript for errors. The folks at Texian Press, including Bill Shirley, Mike Prim, Lane Price and Linda Neckar, helped me through. My assistant, Kathy Tidwell, once more located books for me and worked with my students. World champion secretary Kathryn Pokladnik did her usual fine job in bringing everything together. I am indebted to all these good friends.

Finally, I am grateful to Ellen Fletcher for her friendship and aid, and I am beholden to my father, Frank Welch, for his efforts, without which the books could not be done.

June Rayfield Welch

Irving
October 21, 1977

Table of Contents

Anson Jones, last president of Texas and first Grand Master of Masons in Texas.

Henry Smith Was a Forty-Niner

Henry Smith, born in Kentucky on May 20, 1788, settled in present Brazoria County in 1827. He farmed, surveyed, taught school, and was elected alcalde of the municipality of Brazoria. Of the beginning of the revolution Smith wrote:

> From the passage of the law of the 6th of April [18] 30 the Genl Government [of Mexico] had determined mischief against the colonies. She feared their increasing power and intelligence and had secretly determined to oppress or exterminate. . . . Garrisons were erected commanding all the ports of Texas— and the inmates of all the calabooses of Mexico were turned loose upon us, as soldiers, to fill those Garrisons, comprising in all from 1000 to 1500 of certainly, the most wretched and abandoned set of cutthroats and outlaws that ever made a track on the soil of any country.

Smith sustained a serious head wound in the battle of Velasco. He was a member of the convention which opened on April 1, 1833, the day Santa Anna—who was considered a friend of Texas—became president of Mexico; the delegates resolved that Texas should be separated from Coahuila and appointed Stephen F. Austin to present the resolution and a proposed constitution for the new state to the administration at Mexico City. In 1834 the governor of Coahuila y Texas made Smith the political chief of the new department of the Brazos.

After Santa Anna set aside the Constitution of 1824 and prepared to impose military rule, a consultation was needed to decide what course Texas should follow. When finally Austin got back to Texas, on September 1, 1835, it was possible to have such a meeting. (Austin had been away on his mission for 28 months—a year and a half under Mexican arrest—and Texans had not acted for fear that Santa Anna might retaliate against him.) Austin gave his approval to the Consultation, which had been called by Henry Smith and others.

The delegates began their deliberations on November 3, 1835, a month after the battle of Gonzales. Smith, John Wharton, and Branch Archer wanted an immediate declaration of independence, but on November 6 only fifteen delegates voted to break away from Mexico; 33 wished to remain in the Mexican union and fight to restore the 1824 constitution. On November 12 Henry Smith—with 31 votes to Stephen F. Austin's 22—was chosen provisional governor of the Mexican state of Texas. Smith and James W. Robinson—who received 52 votes for lieutenant governor—were to serve with a council composed of one representative from each of the 13 municipalities. The Consultation sent Austin to the United States to seek aid and appointed Sam Houston to raise an army. Smith and the council, most of whom opposed independence, were soon at odds. After Smith tried to get rid of the council, it attempted to oust him and recognized Robinson as governor; however, Smith pointed out that the action was taken without a quorum and ignored them. As a result both men were trying to govern.

The provisional government, in December, 1835, summoned a March 1 convention to consider the question of independence. As Santa Anna moved his armies into

Henry Smith was the provisional governor from November 14, 1835 to March 1, 1836.

position at the Alamo, William Barret Travis wrote the alcalde at Gonzales, on February 23: "The enemy in large force is in sight. We want men and provisions. Send them to us. We have 150 men and are determined to defend the Alamo to the last." Smith published the message and added

> . . .they have not the provisions nor ammunition to stand more than a thirty day seige at farthest. I call upon you. . .to fly to the aid of your besieged countrymen. . . . The enemy from 6,000 to 8,000 strong are on our border and rapidly moving by forced marches for the colonies.

The determining factor in the Texans' move toward independence was Austin's January 7 letter from New Orleans. Money was needed for defense, but lenders would not finance a civil war because of the slight chance of repayment. Austin wrote:

> Our present position in favor of the republican principles of the Constitution of 1824 can do us no good, and it is doing us harm by deterring that kind of men from joining us that are most useful. . . . With the information now before me, I am in favor of an immediate declaration of independence. Santa Anna was at San Luis Potosi at last accounts, marching on rapidly with a large force against Texas.

Less than 24 hours after the convention met, on March 1, 1836, at Washington-on-the-Brazos, Texas was independent. David G. Burnet's ad interim government succeeded that of Henry Smith, which had been ineffective for several weeks.

Smith polled 741 votes, and Stephen F. Austin had 589, as Sam Houston won the presidency with 4,374 ballots in September, 1836. Henry Smith was the first secretary of the treasury and later was a member of the Fifth Congress. In 1850 he went to California, looking for gold. Although apparently healthy, Smith died in his sleep in a mining camp near Los Angeles on March 4, 1851. His sons, James and John, were

> ten or twelve miles further up the canyon, prospecting for gold, leaving our father and Stewart (his slave) to keep camp. Our provisions were becoming short, I returned for a new supply. On reaching the camp and not seeing my father about, I asked for him. Stewart said he was dead. "Great God!" I exclaimed, "is it possible?" I stepped into the tent, and behold, there lay my father, a lifeless corpse! Stewart said he had been dead two days. . . . He was greatly disappointed in regard to this country. . .

Smith had three marriages. In 1815 he married, in Kentucky, Harriet Gillet, who died five years later, leaving three sons. He then was wed to Elizabeth Gillet, the sister of his first wife, in 1822; she had five daughters and died in a cholera epidemic in 1833. His last wife was Elizabeth Gillet's twin, Sarah, who bore him one daughter and lived until 1863.

After the council attempted to depose Smith, the provisional lieutenant governor, James W. Robinson, tried to carry out the duties of governor from January 11, 1836 to March 1, 1836.

David G. Burnet Lived with the Comanche

The convention summoned by the provisional government met at Washington-on-the-Brazos on March 1, 1836, and Richard Ellis, its president, appointed a committee to draft a declaration of separation from Mexico. The next day George Childress, of Tennessee, presented the independence resolution; upon Sam Houston's motion, it was quickly passed. A constitution was adopted on March 16. On the following morning, about two o'clock, by a vote of 29 to 23, David Gouverneur Burnet was elected—over Samuel Carson, of North Carolina—ad interim president of Texas, which had been "for eighteen years, the land of my peculiar affections. . . ." Lorenzo de Zavala was chosen vice president. Burnet's cabinet was: Secretary of State Samuel P. Carson, Secretary of War Thomas J. Rusk, Secretary of the Treasury Bailey Hardeman, Secretary of the Navy Robert Potter, and Attorney General David Thomas. At the first cabinet meeting, Burnet asked an opinion of T. J. Rusk, who was exhausted from spending three days and nights writing the constitution; the dozing secretary of war awoke and stated, "I think we are in a hell of a fix. . . . Let's go over to the saloon and get a drink, then mount our horses, go fight like the devil, and get out of it."

Upon being warned of the approach of Santa Anna's armies, Burnet ordered a move to Harrisburg, the most accessible point of navigation in the interior. He said, "Let us acquit ourselves like men. . .and by one united, prompt, and energetic exertion, turn back the impotent invader; and planting our standard on the bank of the Rio Grande, dictate to him the terms of mutual recognition."

As Frank Johnson observed, "Burnet's administration was inaugurated at the gloomiest moment of the war." From Harrisburg the capital was moved to Galveston, Velasco, and Columbus. "In the midst of such confusion definite policies were not to be expected. The president simply met problems as they arose and dealt with them as he could."

President Burnet, born April 4, 1788, at Newark, New Jersey, was orphaned in infancy. His father, an army surgeon friend of George Washington, was a member of the Continental Congress; his mother, Gertrude Gouverneur, was related to the Morris family; his older brother, Jacob, was a United States Senator from Ohio. Another brother, Cincinnati mayor Isaac Burnet, and his constituents furnished "The Twin Sisters," the six-pounder cannons used by the Texas Army at San Jacinto.

In 1806 Burnet joined the army of General Francisco de Miranda, who was trying to liberate Venezuela, and served as a lieutenant in two South American campaigns. Enfeebled by tuberculosis he came to Texas in 1817. A. M. Hobby wrote:

> At that time the entire Anglo-American population of this vast country, from the Sabine to the Rio Grande, and from the coast to the Rocky Mountains, did not exceed a hundred souls. From Nacogdoches to San Antonio the smoke of no human habitation arose.

He spent two years on the headwaters of the Colorado River living with the Comanche, and according to Hobby,

David G. Burnet was ad interim president from March 17, 1836 to October 22, 1836.

He slept without shelter through the vicissitudes of the seasons, and subsisted entirely on wild game. The food, exercise and climate of that delightful and invigorating region repaired the wastes of disease, renewed his physical energies and restored him to vigorous health. To the active habits of his hunter life during his stay may be ascribed, not only his cure, but his longevity and subsequent exemption from disease.

After practicing law in Cincinnati he moved to San Felipe de Austin in 1826. At the age of 42 Burnet married Hannah Este in Morristown, New Jersey, and brought her to present Harris County, Texas. Burnet was well-respected; Ashbel Smith thought he was "a man John Knox would have hugged with grim delight." He drew the San Felipe convention's resolutions to separate Texas from Coahuila, and as the supreme judge of the department of the Brazos, in 1834, he conducted the only regular court in colonial Texas.

As president, Burnet had a difficult time. There was no money, and he was always in danger of capture. A large part of the population was in flight, as Houston continued his retreat in spite of Burnet's orders to make a stand. After about a month the government abandoned Harrisburg; Colonel Almonte, who burned the town, nearly caught the Texas president. Mexican troops reached the beach as Burnet was crossing the bay to Galveston Island. Standing in a small boat rowed by two blacks and still within rifle range, Burnet was holding one of his children. Almonte kept his men from firing at the easy target because "there was a mother and children on the boat." About five miles out Burnet boarded the steamboat *Flash* and continued on. Galveston Island was home to about a thousand impoverished refugees; there the Burnets lived in a ragged tent, with two thin blankets serving as bedding for the four of them.

Perhaps Burnet's most important service, in his eight months, was keeping Santa Anna alive. Had renegade soldiers killed him, as they tried to do, Texas would have incurred the disfavor of nations whose friendship was needed. Defense of the Mexican dictator was dangerous; new arrivals from the United States threatened to hang Burnet alongside Santa Anna. Burnet took Santa Anna to Galveston, but since there was no building within which to confine the prisoner, it was necessary to move to Velasco; there two treaties were signed by presidents Burnet and Santa Anna.

In the September, 1836, election Sam Houston became president and M. B. Lamar vice president. Congress met at the new capital, Columbia, on October 3, and Houston succeeded Burnet on October 22. Two years later Burnet became vice president, and when Lamar, on December 12, 1840, left office to convalesce from illness, Burnet was the acting president. Lamar wrote: "I retire, therefore, under the full conviction that the national weal will be promoted while the administration of public affairs remains in your hands. . . ." Burnet turned the government back to Lamar on March 5, 1841.

Whereas he and Lamar were close friends, Burnet challenged Houston to a duel. The election of 1841, in which Houston defeated Burnet for the presidency, was especially bitter. Burnet was Governor J. Pinckney Henderson's secretary of state. Although Burnet opposed secession, when he was elected to the United States Senate after the Civil War the radical Republicans refused to seat him. He had always farmed, working the fields himself and earning a bare living, and he was almost destitute in his last years. Burnet outlived wife and children: his last son was killed in action during the Civil War. He died at Galveston on December 5, 1870. Burnet County and the city of Burnet are named for him.

Burnet first came to Texas because of a lung condition. Living in the open with a band of Comanche, he recovered. He died at the age of 82.

Sam Houston Established His Big Rancho

Within weeks of his January, 1829, marriage to the 18-year-old blonde, blue-eyed Eliza Allen, Sam Houston, 36, returned her to her father's house in Gallatin, Tennessee. He resigned as Tennessee's governor on April 16 and departed for the Cherokee Nation. While living near Fort Gibson, in the Indian Territory, he pondered the future of Texas. Not long after his first journey south of Red River, in 1832, Sam Houston wrote his old friend, President Andrew Jackson, that Texans hoped the United States would purchase the province:

> They are now without laws to govern or protect them. Mexico is involved in Civil War.... The people of Texas are determined to form a State Government and separate from Coahuila, and unless Mexico is soon restored to order and the Constitution revived and reenacted, the Province of Texas will remain separate from the Confederacy of Mexico.

After traveling 500 miles across Texas, Houston declared it to be "the finest country to its extent upon the globe....the country east of the River Grande of the north would sustain a population of ten millions of souls." In the fall of 1835 he was elected to the Consultation by Nacogdoches citizens.

Houston won his San Jacinto victory over Santa Anna in April, 1836, retreating until he believed conditions were favorable. He said, "My policy was to concentrate, retreat and conquer. . . ." The Mexican dictator tried to hide among the common soldiers who had been captured. Recognized and brought before Houston—who had been wounded in the battle—Santa Anna announced, "That man may consider himself born to no common destiny who has conquered the Napoleon of the West. It now remains for him to be generous to the vanquished." Houston replied, "You should have thought of that at the Alamo." When Santa Anna sneered that the new republic was without a governing body and had no flag, Houston stated that Texans believed they had a government and "they will probably be able to make a flag."

Houston made arrangements for protection of the Mexican president from the Texas Army, where the desire for his execution was strong; should Santa Anna be killed, the nations Texas would need as allies might turn against her. With difficulty the badly-wounded Houston—who had to journey to New Orleans for treatment—managed to board the steamer *Yellow Stone*, which was taking President Burnet, his cabinet, and Santa Anna to Galveston. Since he was without funds—he had not been paid—Houston persuaded the captain of the schooner *Flora* to transport him on credit. At New Orleans he received a warm welcome; finally, one month after a bullet shattered his right leg just above the ankle, treatment was begun. On June 4 Houston wrote Lamar: "My wound has improved. Some twenty or more pieces of bone have been taken out of it.... It is only within the last four or five days that I have been able to sit up any portion of the time."

Houston was elected president on September 5, 1836. He attracted 5,199 ballots to Henry Smith's 743 and 587 for Stephen F. Austin. The voters—with only 92 dissents—also approved annexation to the United States if that should become a

President Sam Houston served from October 22, 1836 to December 10, 1838 and from December 13, 1841 to December 9, 1844.

possibility. In his inaugural speech, at Columbia, on October 22, Houston removed his sword but promised to wear it again if Texas ever required a defense.

The new president had to run a government which had no funds or credit and could not really defend itself from attack by Indians or Mexican troops. The standing army offered only slight protection; in fact it constituted a serious threat to the public peace because of lack of discipline, bad morale, and slight interest in any enterprise other than the hanging of Santa Anna. To get the Mexican dictator out of the country in safety, in November, 1836, Houston sent him to Washington upon the pretext that he would urge the United States to recognize Texas. Not only did the captive's departure constitute removal of a local problem, but, as Houston suggested, "Restored to his own country Santa Anna would keep Mexico in commotion for years, and Texas will be safe." Houston wrote Andrew Jackson that Santa Anna was on his way:

> My great desire is that our country Texas shall be annexed to the United States. . . . It is policy to hold out the idea (and few there are who know to the contrary) that we are very able to sustain ourselves against any power who are not important, yet I am free to say to you that we cannot do it. . . . I look to you as the friend and patron of my youth and the benefactor of mankind to interpose in our behalf and save us.

Jackson decided that no effort should then be made toward recognizing Texas. His reluctance was understandable, for the anti-slavery congressmen, who were numerous and hard to ignore, were opposed to the acquisition of Texas. Houston was keenly disappointed, but recognition finally came on March 4, 1837, Andrew Jackson's last day as president.

Houston's solution to his army problem was inspired. Most of the 2,400 men had arrived after San Jacinto; bored, unpaid, and craving the action they had missed, they were easy prey for such demagogues as Felix Huston. The army could not be disbanded because there was no money with which to pay the soldiers. Acting quickly and without notice, Houston furloughed all but 600 men, who would guard against a Mexican invasion. By companies those with furloughs were marched to seaports, where Houston hoped they would take ships to the United States. The army had dissolved before Felix Huston and the other troublemakers realized what was happening.

Two days after Christmas, Secretary of State Stephen F. Austin died. (He had simply worn himself out in the service of Texas.) "The Father of Texas is no more. The first pioneer of the wilderness has departed," wrote Houston.

Since the constitution did not permit Houston to succeed himself, on September 3, 1838, Mirabeau B. Lamar was elected president. Lamar believed that Houston had been written out of his inauguration, but the retiring chief executive was there looking Washington-like in colonial costume and powdered wig. Upon their demand, Houston addressed the spectators. Houston's three-hour-speech held the attention of his auditors but left them with little desire for another oration, even by the new president. Lamar's inaugural address was then read by his secretary.

One of Lamar's objectives was to move the seat of government away from the city named for Houston. The new site was on the Colorado River; Stephen F. Austin had deemed it an appropriate location for a university, and Lamar, on a hunting trip, had admired its beauty. By locating the capital beyond the settlements the Republic would be forced to expand westward, in keeping with Lamar's dream of a Pacific boundary. In May, 1839, work began on the buildings at Austin, and in October the

–Archives Division, Texas State Library

In this Nacogdoches passport record, John M. Dor swears to Samuel Pablo Houston's good character. Ironically, the date was April 21, 1835, exactly a year before Houston's San Jacinto victory. The next certificate, in behalf of Robert Smith, was signed by Houston. Enemies claimed his signature did not read "Sam Houston" but rather "I am Houston."

government moved there from Houston over the objections of East Texas congressman Sam Houston:

> This is the most unfortunate site upon earth for the Seat of Government. . . .It is removed outside of the settlements and not a house between this and Santa Fe. . . . I might have been happy in ignorance at home had I known the full extent of Lamar's stupidity.

The money printed for Lamar's projects had reduced the purchasing power of the dollar to 20¢ by 1841. The Republic had no credit. Late in the year Congress almost dissolved the government, but Houston persuaded the legislators to continue in session. He and David G. Burnet waged a bitter contest for the presidency. As Francis Lubbock noted, Burnet, who had been the acting president for three months, was made the scapegoat for Lamar's administration. Furthermore, Burnet—a genial gentleman, patriot, and scholar—was no match for Houston's personal magnetism and oratory, qualities which then counted heavily in politics. Houston was the victor by a vote of 7,915 to 3,616. Wearing a "linsey-woolsey hunting shirt and pantaloons and an old wide-brimmed white fur hat," Houston was inaugurated December 13, 1841.

When Houston had left office at the close of his first term the public debt was $1.5 million; now it was about $12 million (in gold). Currency of the Republic circulated at 3¢ on the dollar, but the Congress continued to be irresponsible. When the Santa Fe Expedition was captured and its members were imprisoned in Mexico, a resolution was passed—over Houston's veto—annexing California and a tract in Mexico which was greater than the land area of the then United States. Mexican troops made harrassing incursions in 1842, and the Congress passed retaliatory measures, which Houston vetoed or ignored. Responding to invasion demands he explained, "To conquer Mexicans in Texas is one thing—to battle with Mexicans in Mexico is a different kind of warfare. The true interest of Texas is to maintain peace with all nations and cultivate the soil."

Because of Mexican invasions the president moved the capital back to Houston; however, Washington-on-the-Brazos was the seat of government in 1844, when Sam Houston made what he believed would be the successful annexation effort. He wrote Andrew Jackson:

> Now, my venerated friend, you will perceive that Texas is presented to the United States as a bride adorned for her espousal. But if now so confident of the union she should be rejected, her mortification would be indescribable. She has been sought by the United States and this is the third time she has consented. Were she now to be spurned, it would forever terminate expectation on her part. . . .

The attempt did fail. In June, 1844, the United States Senate rejected the treaty, making the annexation of Texas the major issue in the presidential contest, which was won by James K. Polk. In December, President Anson Jones took charge of negotiations. Andrew Jackson had always been concerned about the annexation of Texas. Ashbel Smith wrote:

> In intercourse with Houston running through more than a quarter of a century, I never imagined there was more than one human being to whose judgment he deferred and to which he postponed his own. That man was Andrew Jackson. General Jackson wrote to General Houston more than once urging annexation. . . .

An incident which then occurred is not without significance.... He was leaving Washington-on-the-Brazos for eastern Texas one morning in February, 1845. He came into my private room, booted, spurred, whip in hand. Said he, "Saxe Weimar"—the name of his saddle horse—"is at the door, saddled. I have come to leave Houston's last words with you. If the Congress of the United States should not by the fourth of March pass some measure of annexation which Texas can with honor accede to, Houston will take the stump against annexation for all time to come." When he wished to be emphatic he spoke of himself by name, Houston, in the third person. Without another word, embracing after his fashion, he mounted and left.

On June 6, 1845, Andrew Jackson received a letter—apparently from Houston—with good news about Texas and stated, "All is safe at last." Houston was then on his way to Tennessee, hoping to see the "old Chief" once more. He reached the Hermitage on June 8, three hours after Jackson died. Houston and his young son ran up the stairs, according to Marquis James. Then, holding Sam Houston, Jr., in front of him, General Houston commanded, "Try to remember that you have looked upon the face of Andrew Jackson."

Mirabeau Buonaparte Lamar Dreamed of an Empire

President M. B. Lamar, called by Ashbel Smith a "princely troubador" who "knew not the emotion of personal fear" was described by Francis Lubbock in this fashion:

> He was a man of French type, 5 feet 7 or 8 inches high, with a dark complexion, black hair, inclined to curl, and grey eyes. Lamar was peculiar in his dress; wore his clothes very loose, his pants being of that old style, very baggy and with large pleats, looking odd, as he was the only person I ever saw in Texas in that style of dress. . .rather reserved in conversation. . .however. . .quite companionable with his intimate friends.

Lamar was born August 16, 1798, in Georgia. His family was noted for unusual names; Mirabeau Buonaparte Lamar's nephew was Lucius Quintus Cincinnatus Lamar, Jr., a United States Senator and Supreme Court Justice called "the noblest Mississippian of them all," and a cousin was Gazaway Bugg Lamar. M. B. Lamar was as fond as Sam Houston of the personally theatrical, but he was far more literary. At 21 he published the *Cahawba Press* at the then capital of Alabama: Cahawba, Dallas County. Back in Georgia, as secretary to Governor George M. Troup, he helped entertain the Marquis de Lafayette at Savannah. Although he was a member of the bar, Lamar probably never practiced law.

In 1826 Lamar married Tabitha Jordan, who was seventeen years old; she died of tuberculosis four years later, leaving an infant daughter. He lost an 1833 congressional race, and his newspaper, the *Columbus Enquirer*, failed. Ill and despondent, Lamar moved to Washington County, Texas, in 1835. He stated in a speech made at Washington-on-the-Brazos only days after his arrival, "My advice is to strike for independence and that at once. . . .I hope to see Texas forever free from Mexican domination." Lamar was a rather prolific poet. One of his efforts, published in the *Texas Republican* that October and entitled "The Bride That I Woo is Danger," goes:

> Speed, speed the day when to war I hie!
> The fame of the field is inviting.
> Before my sword shall the foeman fly,
> Or fall in the flash of its lightning.

The other three stanzas are equally bad.

Lamar joined Houston's army as a private, but his performance on the eve of the San Jacinto battle resulted in his promotion to colonel. Philip Graham wrote:

> . . .Lamar rushed to the rescue of Walter P. Lane and Thomas J. Rusk, who had been surrounded by the enemy. Killing one Mexican lancer, and putting the others to flight, Lamar extricated his comrades-in-arms. Legend adds that he then coolly rode in front of the Mexican lines back to his own squad, the enemy acknowledging their admiration by a volley as he passed, and he reining in his horse and bowing in reply.

Lamar commanded the cavalry as Santa Anna's army was routed on April 21. A

Mirabeau Buonaparte Lamar, the second president, served from December 10, 1838 to December 13, 1841.

few days later he became secretary of war. Within a month President Burnet had given him command of the army, but by a margin of eight to one the troops rejected him. Lamar's pride was injured, but resentment of his treatment may have moved Texans to elect him vice president that fall.

As vice president, Lamar made a triumphant visit to Georgia. His reception there and the fame he had won at San Jacinto caused him to run for the presidency. In the middle of a hard-fought campaign his two main opponents committed suicide. Peter William Grayson, on July 9, 1838, at Bean's Station in eastern Tennessee, shot himself, apparently as the result of a disappointment in love. In that same month, James Collinsworth, who had served with Grayson as a commissioner to the United States, drowned himself in Galveston Bay. Lamar trounced Robert Wilson, 6,695 votes to 252, and he and Vice President David G. Burnet were inaugurated on December 10, in the old capitol, which occupied the site of the present Rice Hotel. Houston had about 1,500 people, and the population of the Republic—not counting Indians—was about twenty times that number.

Of the differences between Lamar and Houston, Herbert Gambrell wrote: "While 'Old Sam Jacinto' was holding court in his dirt floor cabin, Lamar gathered about him in the 'White House' of the Republic an entourage which Houston dubbed 'the Court of King Witumpka.' " Because of the bad blood between them, Houston and Lamar narrowly avoided dueling. Philip Graham observed that, "The two men were symbolic of different civilizations: Lamar, of the Old South, its culture and traditions; Houston, of the new frontier of the Southwest in its most victorious mood."

Governor Lubbock cast his judgment in a different fashion:

> Houston's friends believed that General Lamar, while a patriot, honest, and devoted to Texas, was poetical and visionary, without rearing or experience in statecraft, disposed to be extravagant in his ideas of conducting public matters, not appreciating the poverty of the country, in favor of an aggressive policy both against Mexico and the Indians, and that his principal advisers and closest friends were enemies of Houston and his policy, thus binding him to an opposite course.

Lamar's success in warfare—the tiny portion he had experienced—and his impractical bent caused him to dream of conquests that would extend the Republic's limits to the Pacific Ocean. Vice President Burnet said, "Texas proper is bounded by the Rio Grande; but Texas as defined by the sword may comprehend the Sierra Madre. Let the sword do its proper work."

Lamar's temperament was unsuited to solving problems affecting the financial condition of the country. Because Lamar urged that schools be established, he has been considered the father of Texas public education. In 1839 the Congress gave each county three leagues of land in support of its educational efforts, and fifty leagues were set aside to support two universities, the University of Texas and Texas A & M, which were opened much later. Upon Lamar's suggestion, Congress founded the State Library.

Lamar was responsible for moving the capital from Houston. The site commission chose Waterloo, a tiny Colorado River settlement of half a dozen residents; Lamar, on a hunting trip, had been impressed by the location. The commission said the area was "a region worthy of being the home of the brave and free." By the time the government was installed, in October, 1839, the town had been named for Stephen Austin. Congress first met there in November, 1840.

Lamar was also responsible for the military road from La Salle County to Preston Bend on Red River. It would connect several forts. Colonel William G. Cooke commanded the escort accompanying the surveyors through the empty country north of the Brazos. The road crossed the sites of present Waco and Dallas. Fort Johnson and Fort Preston, a supply post, were built in Grayson County near Holland Coffee's trading post.

Lamar's aggressive Indian policy, which included expulsion of the Cherokee from East Texas, provoked new depredations. At the Council House Fight, in San Antonio, both whites and Indians suffered heavy casualties. The Comanche were moved to revenge, and a huge war party of perhaps 1,000 braves raided as far south as Victoria.

Because of illness, on December 12, 1840, Lamar turned over his duties to Vice President Burnet. Colonel James Morgan wrote of the Republic's plight:

> We have a bad state of affairs here now—Lamar the poor imbecile could not hold out and had to give up the helm of state to Burnet—who is even more worthless—. . .Ole Sam H. with all his faults appears to be the only man for Texas—He is still unsteady—intemperate but drunk in a ditch is worth a thousand of Lamar and Burnet. . . .

Having recovered, Lamar took over as chief magistrate on March 5, 1841, and began planning to send representatives to Santa Fe to demonstrate sovereignty over that part of the Republic which is now eastern New Mexico. Leaving in June, the Santa Fe Expedition, composed of 321 men, got lost. After many hardships they were arrested, and the survivors were imprisoned in Mexico. They—and veterans of the Mier Expedition, who were also incarcerated there—did not get back to Texas for years; some never did.

Houston's second inauguration as president took place at Austin's old wooden capitol on December 13, 1841. Lamar retired to his Richmond farm; he was living there when his sixteen-year-old daughter, Rebecca, died in Georgia.

During the Mexican War Lamar was Zachary Taylor's inspector general. After seeing action at Monterrey, he was relegated to—by Senator Houston's influence, he believed—a camp at Laredo.

In 1851 Lamar married Henrietta Maffitt; she was 24, and he was 53. Their daughter, Loretto, was born the following year. Although he was in constant financial difficulty, Lamar published, in 1857, his book of poems, *Verse Memorials*. About that time he complained: "For many months I have had use for five or six dollars which I have not been able to raise, except by the slow process of selling a little butter which my wife saved from a few cows." Fortunately, President James Buchanan made him the American minister to Nicaragua and Costa Rica, and his $10,000-a-year salary allowed him to pay some old debts. Burnet's letter congratulating him on the appointment included this reflection: "My own condition is at present painfully embarrassing, and I have not the means of making a decent living for my family." After twenty months in South America Lamar returned to Texas on October 10, 1859, had a heart attack on December 18, and died the next morning. Mrs. Lamar died near Santa Anna, Coleman County, on October 6, 1891; she was buried beside her husband in the Masonic Cemetery at Richmond. Lamar County is named for him, as is Lamar University and a major street in nearly every Texas town.

19

Anson Jones Was a Physician

Anson Jones, whose father fought in the battle of Bunker Hill, was born at Great Barrington, Massachusetts, on January 20, 1798. He was better educated than most of the leaders of the Republic. Jones' father, especially concerned about the future of this youngest of ten children, insisted that he should have a profession. After three years of study, Jones was licensed as a physician in Onieda, New York. Because his practice developed slowly, he entered Jefferson Medical College and graduated in 1827. For five years he practiced in Philadelphia with only slight success; then moving to New Orleans, he "found the pernicious habits of gambling...growing upon me...I also found myself learning to imitate the fashionable habit of taking a 'julip' much oftener than was at all necessary."

In October, 1833, he landed in Texas, immediately discovered his mistake, and planned an early return to New Orleans. With assets of only $17 cash and about $50 worth of medicine, Jones had debts exceeding $2,000. While waiting for the ship upon which he was to leave Texas, he was persuaded to hang out his shingle at Brazoria. Later he wrote:

> My sole and exclusive object was to find a suitable field for the exercise of my profession and to make myself useful...in this new and young country of my adoption.

Jones did well, and by 1835 he had, according to his reckoning,

> a practice worth in money and available property about five thousand dollars a year, with a prospect of its increasing; and had I continued at my business, and not been induced to join the army and go into public life, I might and probably would at this time have been worth an independent fortune, and as wealthy as any man in Texas. . . .

After the Alamo fell, and when the Runaway Scrape was at high tide, Jones joined the army. While assigned to a medical unit he insisted upon remaining a private soldier. He became a close friend of Sam Houston and fought at San Jacinto. Prior to the battle, in conversation with Houston

> He asked me after supper, privately, what I thought of the prospect. I told him the men were deserting and if the retreating policy were continued much longer he would be pretty much alone. He seemed thoughtful and irresolute. Said he hoped yet to get a bloodless victory.

Congressman Jones was somewhat unpopular because he opposed making Houston the capital. In 1838 President Houston sent him to Washington to represent the Republic. As senator from Brazoria County he called Lamar "a sort of political troubador and crusader and wholly unfit for...the everyday realities of his present station." To the same diary Jones confided: "No man is more completely master of the art of appropriating to himself the merit of others' good acts. . .than General Houston."

Houston, again becoming president in 1842, made Anson Jones his secretary of state. Acquisition of Texas had become a major political issue in the United States and

President Anson Jones served from December 9, 1844 to February 19, 1846 when he lowered the Lone Star Flag of the Republic.

would result in James K. Polk's election about the time Jones was defeating—by about 1,500 votes—General Edward Burleson for the Texas presidency. Jones, Sam Houston's candidate, took office December 4, 1844. His main task was achieving annexation. Because of the caution he was forced to exercise in public statements, critics charged him with blocking annexation. Anson Jones presented, on June 6, 1845, "the propositions which have been made on the part of the United States," which were accepted by the Texas Congress. A convention met on July 4 and, by a vote of 55 to 1, passed an annexation ordinance; the dissenter was Richard Bache, the grandson of Benjamin Franklin. Six other delegates did not vote. Even though Texas, under his direction, became part of the United States, Anson Jones was ruined politically by suspicions that he had opposed annexation. He never regained his former high position in public esteem.

It was Jones who pronounced the death of the Republic on February 16, 1846, at the Austin capitol, which had been used as a church, school, and annexation convention hall since the House and Senate had last met there, in February, 1842. Jones said:

> The Lone Star of Texas, which ten years ago arose amid clouds over fields of carnage, obscurely seen for awhile, has culminated, and following an inscrutable destiny, has passed on and become fixed forever in that glorious constellation which all free men and lovers of freedom in the world must reverence and adore—the American Union.... The final act in the great drama is now performed. The Republic of Texas is no more!

As Jones lowered the flag of the Republic, its pole broke.

Jones was the first master of Texas' first Masonic lodge: Holland Lodge Number 36, at Brazoria, chartered in March, 1836. As Mexican troops menaced Brazoria, Jones took the charter away in his saddle bags. Holland Lodge was reopened at Houston in 1837. When the Grand Lodge of Texas was organized, with Sam Houston presiding, Anson Jones was chosen as the grand master.

After his retirement Anson Jones farmed near Washington-on-the-Brazos. Upon the death of T. J. Rusk and because of the legislature's disavowal of Houston, Jones hoped to be elected senator, but he was ignored. In 1838 Jones had written in his diary:

> Collinsworth's drowning himself was a thing of course. I had expected it, as I knew him to be deranged, and while excited, almost mad. I shall be surprised at no one's committing suicide after hearing of Colonel Grayson's doing so. It is the first time in my life that anyone in the circle of my acquaintance has done such an act, and it has shocked me more than the death of a dozen others would have done in the usual course.

On January 9, 1858, in Houston's old Capitol Hotel, the building that had housed the government of the Republic, Jones killed himself. Earlier he had told a friend, "Here in this house, twenty years ago, I commenced my political career in Texas, and here I would like to close it." His widow, Mary Smith Jones, died fifty years later in Houston on the last day of 1907.

Jones County is named for him, and Anson is the county seat.

Governors of the State of Texas

Sam Houston in Masonic apron.

Henderson Led the Texans off to War

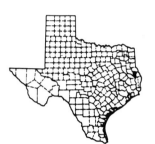

James Pinckney Henderson was the first governor of the new state of Texas. He was born near Lincolnton, North Carolina, March 31, 1808, and after graduating from Chapel Hill College he studied law and was admitted to the bar in 1829. Henderson was

> one of those magnetic men that impress you at first sight as being of no ordinary stamp. He was tall and rather delicate in appearance, with light hair, fair complexion, and fine grey eyes; affable, and sparkling all over with genuine vivacity.

In 1830 he became the aide-de-camp to the major general of North Carolina militia. Henderson's health had been damaged by overwork while reading law eighteen hours a day, and, in 1835, he moved to Canton, Madison County, Mississippi in hopes of recovering from his lung condition. He quickly attained a position of leadership; at a meeting called to stimulate sympathy for the people of Texas, Henderson's oratory impressed United States Senator Foote, who wrote:

> His appearance was noble and commanding; his eyes and whole countenance flashed forth the light of commingling thought and passion, and he swept the audience before him like a whirlwind.

Upon learning of Santa Anna's invasion, in the spring of 1836, Henderson raised a company of Mississippians which Captain David Fulton took to Texas. When Henderson arrived, President Burnet commissioned him to recruit troops in the United States. In Tennessee and North Carolina were plenty of volunteers, but he had no funds for their transportation; only one company, a North Carolina outfit, reached Texas, at Henderson's personal expense.

Even though he was among those who demanded Santa Anna's execution in the early days of the Republic, Houston appointed him attorney general and—after the death of Stephen F. Austin—secretary of state. At the age of 29, Henderson became the minister to England and France, charged with obtaining the recognition of Texas' independence and negotiating commercial treaties. He made trading agreements with Britain, but anti-slavery sentiment in Parliament rendered recognition impossible. The French sent an agent to determine whether recognition was warranted; Count Alphonse de Saligny—who would later fight "the Pig War" with Austin innkeeper Richard Bullock—made a favorable report, and Louis Philippe recognized the independence of Texas.

In October, 1839, Henderson married, in London, nineteen-year-old Frances Cox, of Philadelphia, whose family was living in Paris when he met her. She was fluent in eighteen languages and competent in seven others. Henderson took her to a log house in San Augustine, where he opened a law office, in 1840, and hoped to repair his finances. (The Republic could not reimburse Henderson's expenses for his three-year sojourn.) He was urged to run for the presidency to succeed Lamar, but he was not yet 35, as required by the constitution. The response of his friends, that he appeared to be at least forty, must have been a comfort.

James Pinckney Henderson, the first governor, served from February 19, 1846, to December 21, 1847; however, from May 19 to sometime in November of 1846 Lieutenant Governor A. C. Horton acted as governor while Henderson served as a Mexican War major general.

When, in 1844, President Houston asked Henderson to assist Isaac Van Zandt in negotiating an annexation treaty, he accepted. Secretary of State John Calhoun recommended the treaty, but the Senate rejected it. The Americans reacted by making James K. Polk president and annexing Texas.

Henderson was a member of the Constitutional Convention of 1845. The leading contenders for governor were Dr. James B. Miller and Anson Jones' vice-president, Kenneth Anderson. A native of Henderson's North Carolina hometown, Anderson was the law partner of Henderson and T. J. Rusk. During the campaign he died at Fanthorp, which was renamed Anderson in his honor. Henderson then entered the race and defeated Miller by taking 7,853 of 9,578 votes cast. Governor Henderson never moved his family to Austin.

The first battle of the Mexican War was fought on April 25, 1846, near present Brownsville, and General Zachary Taylor asked for four Texas regiments of six-month volunteers. The legislature, on May 9, authorized the governor to lead the Texans, and on the 19th Henderson notified Lieutenant Governor Albert Clinton Horton:

> I shall this day leave the seat of government to take command of the Texas forces raised under the requisition of General Taylor and shall move beyond the Rio Grande into Mexico. Under these circumstances, you are required by the Constitution to act as governor of the state....

General Henderson commanded the second Texas regiment on the third day of the battle of Monterrey, and General Taylor appointed Henderson, W. J. Worth, and Jefferson Davis to negotiate terms of the Mexican surrender. Congress voted him a $1,500 sword for his valor. Henderson resumed his duties in Austin on December 13, 1846; he refused to accept any salary from the state for the period of his military service. He did not seek reelection as governor; after leaving office Henderson returned to his San Augustine practice.

Judge Norman Kittrell wrote that once, when Henderson was attending court in another county, a man threatened to kill him. Henderson told a friend that he had done the man no harm. The friend replied, "He will kill you all the same." Henderson said, "I have a family to support.... What shall I do?" His friend stated, "Kill him."

Kittrell wrote,

> the General acted upon the tragic suggestion and "removed" the man who was preparing to assassinate him; and calmly proceeded to the courthouse and entered upon the trial of a case. He was justified both by public sentiment and the law and no reproach attached to his action.

Upon the death of his old partner, Senator T. J. Rusk, Henderson was elected to the Senate. He began his service on November 9, 1857, and died in Washington on June 4, 1858. His body was moved to the Texas State Cemetery in 1930. One of Henderson's daughters married a Prussian nobleman, and most of his descendants lived in Europe—none in Texas—in 1931. Henderson County bears his name, as does the Rusk County seat.

Contemporaries called Henderson "the elegant J. Pinckney."

George T. Wood Was a Just Man

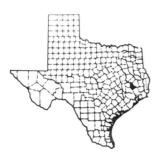

George T. (for Thomas or, perhaps, Tyler) Wood was born March 12, 1795, near Cuthbert, Georgia; his father died when he was five years old. Wood raised a company during the Creek War and fought at the battle of Horseshoe Bend, where, according to family tradition, he met Sam Houston and Edward Burleson. As governor, Wood was six feet tall, weighed 200 pounds, had greying black hair, and refused to wear socks. Francis Lubbock remembered him as "a good-looking man, and was of more than medium height; well formed, strong and vigorous in appearance."

In 1837 Wood started to New York City to buy stock for his store in Cuthbert. At the Georgia capital, Milledgeville, he met Martha Gindrat, a widow with three children. They were married that fall. In 1839 Wood brought his family—which included David, Henry, and Elizabeth Gindrat and a new daughter, Martha Anne Wood—and about 30 slaves belonging to his wife, to Galveston by water from Fort Gaines, Georgia. Accompanying them was a freedman, Uncle Tony, who had adopted Wood as his guardian and was "supported, though never known to do any work except fishing in the 107 years of his life." Wood cleared a plantation just west of the Trinity near Point Blank in present San Jacinto County. Of the five children born there, two died in childhood, as did the first child, Martha Anne.

Wood was elected to the Congress of the Republic in 1841; then, in 1845, he served in the annexation convention. When the Mexican War began he resigned from the state Senate to raise a company of the Second Texas Mounted Volunteers. He served as regimental colonel from July 4 to October 1, 1846, when the unit was dissolved. In Mexico he and Colonel Jefferson Davis, the commander of a Mississippi regiment, became close friends, but Wood had trouble with Major General J. P. Henderson, who had taken leave as governor of Texas. The incident which produced the hard feelings was trivial but had significant consequences. The *Texas Democrat*, in December, 1846, announced:

> We are requested by Gov. Henderson to state that the report of Col. Wood's published in the Telegram. . .and purporting to have been made to Gen. Henderson, was not received by him as it was published. Col. Wood... sent in the report, in the first place, as published, which Gen. Henderson refused to receive, after reading it, upon the ground that it was disrespectful to himself, inasmuch as Col. Wood, in that report, spoke of receiving his orders to move his regiment directly from Gen. Taylor, when in fact the orders for the movement of his regiment were given by Gen. Henderson himself. . . . Another cause of the refusal of Gen. Henderson to receive the report was that the report did not recognize Gen. Henderson as having led that regiment into the city of Monterrey as the superior officer, which he did, and commanded it throughout the day.

Those who served under Wood admired him for his valor at Monterrey, and resentment toward Henderson may have resulted in Wood's success in his race for governor.

George T. Wood, the second governor, served from December 21, 1847 to December 21, 1849.

In the 1847 gubernatorial contest, Wood polled 7,154 votes to J. B. Miller's 5,106, and N. H. Darnell's 1,276. J. J. Robinson and others had 1,231 ballots. (Isaac Van Zandt, a leading candidate, died during the campaign.) O. M. Roberts wrote:

> Colonel Wood had the advantage over his competitors from having recently been in the army with three Texas regiments, and a number of the companies in his own regiment had volunteered from Eastern Texas. To show what small influence exerted weight in those days it was humorously said that Governor Henderson made Wood governor of the State by omitting to mention the latter's gallant conduct in the report of the battle of Monterrey, which apparent slight aroused the resentment of the Texas soldiers to such an extent that they actually elected him governor out of revenge and as a reward for his courageous career in Mexico.

During Wood's term there was much controversy over Texas' northwestern limits. The territory acquired by the United States at the close of the Mexican War included areas claimed by Texas in present New Mexico and Colorado. Since the federal government was unwilling to acknowledge Texas' sovereignty over the territory east of the Rio Grande, Wood asked the legislature for troops to enforce the state's rights. After he left office, Wood, as a private citizen, journeyed to Washington to assist in the boundary settlement, which was part of the Compromise of 1850.

Wood's 1849 reelection bid was frustrated by Peter Hansbrough Bell, who received 10,319 votes to Wood's 8,764 and John T. Mills' 2,632. Wood blamed his loss on the failure of Houston—who lived about five miles away—to make adequate efforts in his behalf, for much of Wood's opposition was because of his long friendship with the senator. An observer wrote: "These men will move heaven and earth to defeat Wood, if for no other cause, simply to cripple Houston in this State." Another factor was Bell's popularity, which came from his being an Indian fighter and a veteran of San Jacinto and the Mexican War.

Mrs. Wood managed the plantation during her husband's term in Austin. Governor Wood lived at Bullock's Hotel and came home as often as possible, usually by mule. Upon leaving office he moved five miles up the Trinity to a new place; but after the death of the youngest child, Wood decided it was unhealthy to live so close to the water. He began building a great house two miles from the river on a hill named for an Indian chief—Ben Ash—who had lived there. When asked why he was constructing such a large house, Wood said it was for his friends. His daughter, who was fifteen years old when he died, said she never recalled a meal without guests. The house was still unfinished at his death, on September 3, 1858. Mrs. Wood survived until January 5, 1861. They were buried on their original plantation.

Apparently Wood was admitted to the bar, but he never practiced law. His daughter remembered the scars on his legs from wounds received in the Creek War. She said he was always "laughing, jesting, and sustaining a mirthful atmosphere wherever he might be. He was kind and indulgent to family, slaves, and neighbors, indeed to all the world." Wood's favorite mount was his mule, Pantalette. While on a long journey he simply tied Pantalette to his leg at night and used his saddle for a pillow. His slaves regularly cultivated the fields of a destitute neighbor; when Wood died the unfortunate told Mary Wood, "Well, daughter, the poor man's friend is gone." His epitaph reads, "Here sleeps a just man." Woodville, the seat of Tyler County, and Wood County were named for him.

TEXAS BEFORE THE COMPROMISE OF 1850

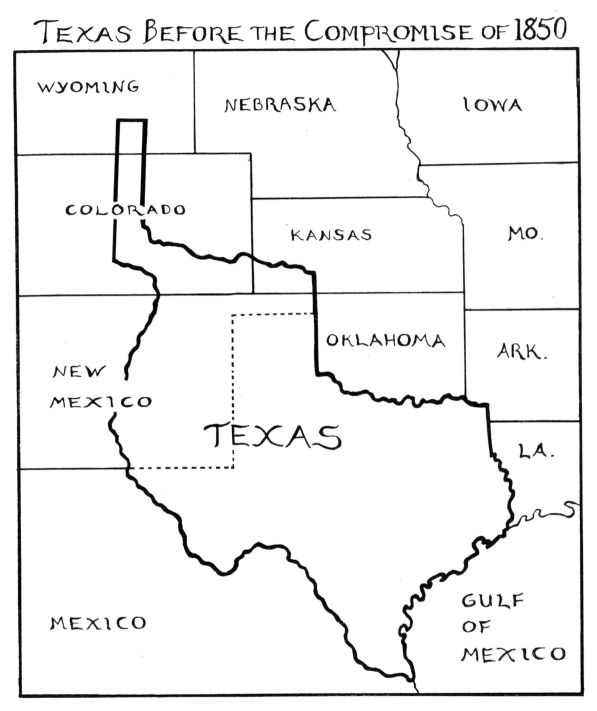

–Lynn H. Guier

As part of the Compromise of 1850 Texas sold territory extending as far north as Wyoming.

Peter Bell Had not an Enemy in Texas

Peter Hansbrough Bell, twice governor and twice a Texas congressman, spent his last 41 years in North Carolina. Francis Lubbock called him

> a Virginian—a fine type of southern gentleman, a well-built, handsome young fellow when he landed in Texas. He displayed much pluck and determination in participating as a private in the battle of San Jacinto. He was always affable and kind; became popular; rose rapidly in public estimation; commanded a company of rangers at an early day; fought bravely at Monterrey as lieutenant-colonel in Wood's regiment, and then became Governor of Texas.

Tall and slender and with his black hair collar-length, in Ranger dress Bell, booted, spurred, and wearing a broad sombrero, had two pistols and a Bowie knife at his belt, but in town he was "elegant and dignified." John Henry Brown considered him "distinguished by kind and genial characteristics. It is believed he had not a personal enemy in Texas."

Bell was born March 11, 1808, in Culpeper County, Virginia. He came to Texas in 1836 and fought at San Jacinto with Henry Karnes' company. Remaining in the army, he became the inspector general in 1839. He joined John Coffee Hays' Rangers and was a major in the Somervell Expedition. Just prior to the Mexican War Bell was a Ranger captain at Corpus Christi; his 47-man company was the first Texas unit to join Zachary Taylor's army. Bell won praise for his part in the battle of Buena Vista, and he then commanded that part of Hays' regiment assigned to Texas for service on the Rio Grande.

Bell won the governorship from George Wood in 1849. He was as positive as Wood had been about Texas' ownership of territory in present New Mexico and Colorado; however, Bell did show some willingness to sell the area. In 1850 Robert S. Neighbors was sent to organize the new counties of Presidio, El Paso, Worth, and Santa Fe. The northwestern Texas boundary was an important national question because it provided another opportunity to argue the extension of slavery. C. C. Mills advised Bell:

> The House of Representatives is not yet organized. It is a crisis in our affairs, and what it will result in, God only knows. There is but little disposition on the part of the southern members to bear with northern encroachment any longer and there is evidently a determination on the part of many of them to engage in no legislation until the question is settled, and if the present Congress does not settle it I am of opinion that the South will never meet the North again in general Council. Texas having so recently come into the Union, should not be foremost to dissolve it; but I trust she will not waver, when the crisis shall come.

American troops frustrated Neighbors' attempts to assert Texan authority at Santa Fe, thereby aiding those who intended to establish a new state on soil claimed by Texas. Bell asked the legislature for troops to occupy Santa Fe and "quell the rebellious spirit now prevailing there, and to enable us to firmly establish the

Peter Bell, the third governor, served from December 21, 1849 to November 23, 1853.

jurisdiction of the state over it." A joint legislative committee resolved "that Texas will maintain the integrity of her Territory at all hazard and to the last extremity." There was support for sending 3,000 Rangers to Santa Fe. The *State Gazette* said: "In the whole course of our long residence in Texas we have never seen among the people so much unanimity and enthusiasm as prevails at this time...upon the subject of the enforcement of our jurisdiction over Santa Fe." Mississippi offered to help Texas if a war broke out.

Zachary Taylor's death, on July 9, released some of the tension. Texans had resented his position on the boundary issue, and the new president, Millard Fillmore, favored a settlement. Maryland Senator James Pearce's bill, which established the present boundary, was passed with the approval of senators Houston and Rusk. The Texas legislature gave up any claim to some 56 million acres west and north of that line in return for $10,000,000 in United States securities; not only did the arrangement solve the boundary problem, it also provided funds for payment of the state's public debt.

Another important question presented in Bell's first term concerned the seat of government. Austin was only the temporary capital; an election was to be held on the question of location in 1850, and twenty seven years later Texans were to vote on the permanent seat of government. In March, Austin, with 7,674 votes, prevailed over Palestine, with 1,854, and Tehuacana, with 1,143. When the permanent election was held, in 1872, Austin attracted 15,355 more votes than the other nominees—Houston and Waco—combined.

Bell was reelected in 1851. The vote count was: Peter Bell, 13,595; M. T. Johnson, 5,262; John Greer, 4,061; B. H. Epperson, 2,971; and T. J. Chambers, 2,320. Near the end of his term, in 1853, Governor Bell resigned. He had won the congressional seat of Volney Howard, who earlier fought duels with Hiram Runnels and another Mississippi governor before coming to Texas and who had now been appointed to a federal position in California. Bell was succeeded by Lieutenant Governor James W. Henderson.

On March 3, 1857, Congressman Bell married the wealthy Mrs. Ella Reeves Eaton Dickens; upon completing his second term he moved to her Littleton, North Carolina, home. They were impoverished by the loss of their slaves in the Civil War. Jim Hogg learned of Bell's poverty in 1891 and suggested that he be pensioned. The legislature then voted to grant the 83-year-old former governor $100 a year for life. He died in March 8, 1898, a few months after his wife. Their remains were later moved from Littleton to the Texas State Cemetery. Bell County is named for him.

The statue of Peter Bell stands beside the Bell County capitol in Belton.

"Smoky" Henderson Was too Late to Fight

James Wilson Henderson was elected lieutenant governor in 1851. He became governor by virtue of Peter Bell's resignation to enter Congress, and he served from November 23 to December 21, 1853.

Henderson, born August 15, 1817, in Tennessee, was inspired by Travis' call for aid. He raised a company of fifty volunteers but the battle of San Jacinto was fought before they got to Texas. President Burnet sent the 19-year-old Captain Henderson to the United States on recruiting duty. After settling in Harris County, Henderson became the county surveyor and was admitted to the bar.

Naturally, Henderson was compared with Peter Bell, whom De Shields considered "the most unique and interesting figure" in Texas history. He was also measured by the virtues of the other Henderson; De Shields believed he paled beside "the elegant and affable J. Pinckney Henderson, being rather crude and careless in his manners and dress."

Francis Lubbock wrote: "J. W. was called by the familiar sobriquet of 'Smoky' to distinguish him from the elegant J. Pinckney." The nickname came from a story Henderson told about his uncle, "Smoky" Wilson. When his son ran for office, "Smoky" Wilson—conscious of local prejudice against attorneys—told friends not to be reluctant about voting for the boy, since he was not *much* of a lawyer.

Henderson was a fine trial attorney who "seemed never to have forgotten any principle of law heard asserted and usually remembered the volume that it was cited from." A steadfast friend of Sam Houston, Henderson was elected to Congress over James Morgan, in 1843, and was chairman of the House committee on annexation. In 1847 he bested Mirabeau B. Lamar to become the speaker.

Afer secession Henderson commanded a Confederate company stationed on the Texas coast. He was a delegate to the 1866 constitutional convention and later helped break Governor E. J. Davis' hold on Texas. By his marriage to Laura Hooker, he had two sons; after her death he married Sophia Price, who bore him three children. He died in Houston, on August 30, 1880, and was buried by Holland Lodge, which he and Anson Jones had both served as master.

One day in 1861, as Oran Roberts presided over the Secession Convention upstairs in the capitol, Henderson stopped by Governor Houston's first floor office. Houston had fought those who advocated secession and was about to lose that battle. Paraphrasing Kittrell's account in places, the governor "with the deliberation and clear enunciation that characterized his speech, said, 'Well—Henderson—what—can—I—do—for—you—my—friend?' "

Henderson said, "Governor, I want you to pardon Mrs. Monroe."

"Why should I pardon her?. . .Wasn't she fairly tried?"

"Yes, and given six years."

"And she appealed and the conviction was affirmed, Henderson? Am I right?"

"Yes. . .the opinion. . .was the ablest ever written by Judge Roberts."

"Oran Milo Roberts? That fellow who is presiding over that mob upstairs?"

"Yes, governor."

"Then I'll pardon her. No citizen shall be deprived of liberty by such a fellow."

After Peter Bell resigned to enter Congress, James Wilson Henderson became the fourth governor and served the balance of Bell's term, from November 23, 1853 to December 21, 1853.

E. M. Pease Knew All the Laws of Texas

Elisha Marshall Pease was the first three-term governor. Francis Lubbock called him "a fine constitutional lawyer, a great statesman, and a patriot of incorruptible integrity. Besides this, Pease was wide-awake and progressive in his views of public policy."

Born at Enfield, Connecticut, on January 3, 1812, Pease attended Westfield Academy until, at the age of fourteen, he went to work in a general store. For four years he was a postal clerk at Hartford; then, in 1835, he came to Texas from New Orleans with D. C. Barrett. They settled at Bastrop—then called Mina—where Pease studied law under Barrett.

Barrett was chairman and Pease secretary of Mina's committee of public safety, the first in Texas. The committee, formed to handle Indian defense, was soon concerned with the problem of Santa Anna. Pease and Barrett were members of the peace faction at a July, 1835, meeting in San Felipe where the delegates met to assess the condition of the country. Santa Anna's troops were on the way, and the war party was demanding the seizure of San Antonio. When the arrests of Lorenzo de Zavala, William Barret Travis, and others were ordered, the war party's position seemed to be vindicated; the Texans would have to fight or submit to Santa Anna's demands.

Word reached Mina, on September 27, that Mexican troops were en route to seize a cannon that had been given to Gonzales settlers for Indian protection. Pease was among the volunteers who participated in the minor battle at Gonzales that started the Revolution. In November, he became secretary to the council of the provisional government. He was clerk of the committee which wrote the constitution of the Republic, and he drafted the ordinance establishing the ad interim government, for which he labored in the navy and treasury departments. As Benjamin Miller pointed out:

> No other man was officially connected with so many phases of its development from the organization of the Mina committee to the inauguration of the regular constitutional government, with Houston as the regularly chosen president. If any man knew at first hand the evolution of the government of the Republic of Texas completely, that man was E. M. Pease.

His services continued as the Congress met at Columbia on October 3, 1836. Pease was the secretary of the House committee that drew the laws creating the courts and county offices; and he drafted the judiciary act. He was a congressman, a senator, and the comptroller of Houston's first presidency. After annexation Pease wrote the state's probate code. In 1883 the *Austin Daily Statesman* repeated a belief that E. M. Pease knew every detail of every law passed from statehood to the Civil War.

Because of a minor speech impediment, Pease allowed partners to try his lawsuits; his strength lay in research and pleading. In 1850 he returned from a Connecticut vacation with a bride, the former Lucadia Niles. The journey to her new home took nearly two months. Her carriage was the first in Brazoria, and their home was the first to have a front sidewalk, a flower bed, and no weeds in the yard. Brazorians had always left the grounds around their homes untended.

Elisha Pease, the fifth governor, was also the thirteenth governor. His terms were December 21, 1853 to December 21, 1857 and August 8, 1867 to September 30, 1869.

In 1851 Pease announced, half-heartedly, against Governor Bell, who had offended those who wanted Houston to be the capital. Bell and two others had counted the votes that kept the seat of government at Austin for the next twenty years and Houston partisans charged fraud. Pease withdrew from the race after realizing that opposition to fellow Democrat Bell would simply elect the Whig B. H. Epperson. Until this election, party affiliation was not important. Texas had always gone Democratic because the party of Jackson and Polk had sponsored annexation.

In 1853 Pease announced for governor again. T. J. Chambers, M. T. Johnson, J. W. Dancy, and former governor Wood were among his Democratic opponents. Because of the strength of the Whig W. B. Ochiltree, Johnson decided that Democrats should offer a single candidate; he withdrew and endorsed Pease, who led the balloting. Ochiltree was second and Wood third.

As governor, Pease's first interest was education. Until then only Galveston had levied a school tax. The state had never supported schools, which were operated by individuals, churches, and lodges. The 1845 constitution provided for public education; 10% of state taxes was to go into a school fund, and each county was given four leagues of land for school purposes. Pease got the legislature to set aside $2 million in United States bonds—which had been received in 1850 for land in present New Mexico—and the money in the state school fund as a perpetual endowment. Interest from that endowment would be distributed among the counties according to the number of children between the ages of five and sixteen.

There was difficulty in obtaining railroad service. Prospective builders seemed more interested in the quantity of land they would get from the state than with operating trains. Pease reminded the legislature, in 1855, that progress under past programs had been slight. Only three companies were engaged in construction, and after years of offering up to sixteen acres per mile, only twelve miles of track had been laid. To stimulate building the state began lending $6,000 for each mile of rail.

Indians were a problem, as always. Pease ordered Captain James Callahan to raise a company of mounted volunteers for the protection of the Guadalupe River settlements, which the Indians had ravaged. He was to pursue hostiles wherever the trails led. Anxious to stop some Lipan Apache who were raiding from Mexico, Callahan obtained permission from the Piedras Negras commandant to pursue war parties across the Rio Grande; however, he was not to enter any Mexican town. In September, 1855, Callahan, with about 115 men, pursued some Lipan raiders from Bexar County to the border. When the Indians continued into Mexico, Callahan crossed the river near Eagle Pass. They were surrounded by 700 Indians and some Mexicans commanded by a Captain Manchaca. Callahan led a charge through the enemy's lines, reformed, and charged back into the circle. Callahan lost four men, but the Indians and their allies withdrew after sustaining more than 100 casualties. That night Callahan was beseiged by Manchaca in Piedras Negras; he finally got his men across the river after setting fire to the town.

The United States Army, afraid Callahan might have touched off a border war, complained to Pease, who backed the pursuit but disapproved of Callahan's actions at Piedras Negras. Pease said he would not want war on the border, but it was the federal government's failure to protect the frontier that made volunteer troops necessary.

The American Party, or Know Nothings, in June, 1855, held a convention at Washington-on-the-Brazos and nominated Lieutenant Governor David C. Dickson to contest Pease. Even though Pease was reelected, 25 Know Nothings won places in the legislature. He was the first governor to live in the Mansion.

Pease was the first governor to occupy the Mansion at Austin.

Hardin Runnels Defeated Sam Houston

Hardin Richard Runnels, the only man who ever bested Sam Houston in an election, was born in Mississippi on August 30, 1820. He, his two brothers, and their mother opened a Bowie County, Texas plantation about 1842. (His Uncle Hiram, a Mississippi governor, fought a duel with Volney Howard, caned Mississippi governor McNutt, was an annexation convention delegate, and had Runnels County named for him.) Hardin Runnels, after three terms in the legislature, became speaker of the House and then lieutenant governor.

The 1856 Democratic State Convention commended Senator Rusk and congressmen George Smyth and Peter Bell on their support of the Kansas-Nebraska Act, but it "most decidedly" disapproved "the vote of Senator Houston." Aware that the legislature would not return him to the Senate—and this was prior to election of senators by popular vote—Houston flirted with the Know Nothings, who carried only one state—Maryland—in 1856 and soon disappeared. Know Nothing popularity in Texas was not due to anti-Catholicism and nativism so much as the party's Unionist stance. The new Republican party had no appeal for Texans because of its abolitionist cast.

In 1857 the Democrats met in Waco's Baptist church and nominated Hardin Runnels for governor. The *Huntsville Recorder*—under the headline "Old Sam in the Field"—stated that Houston, calling himself a Jackson Democrat, was running as an independent. Alluding to the convention, Houston—who pronounced Waco the way the Indians did—referred to "that struggling village of Wah-Ko, which is always trying to upset my plans." The nominee for lieutenant governor, Francis Lubbock, noted that everyone understood that Runnels "would not attempt a thorough canvass. He might visit some localities in a quiet way, but he would not make speeches. . . .he was not a popular speaker."

Runnels overwhelmed Houston, 38,552 to 23,628. He warned that:

> Year by year the South is becoming weaker, the North growing stronger. The equilibrium has been destroyed which afforded the only sure and permanent guarantee of protection against abolition innovation. . . . I do not hesitate to believe that the determination of Texas will be taken to assume the guardianship of her own destinies and bid adieu to a connection no longer consistent with the rights, dignity, and honor of an equal and independent State. . . . No reasonable effort should be spared to secure that military organization and training indispensable to the liberties of every free State. . . .

During Runnels' term the Indians were troublesome and Juan Cortina was ravaging the border. John S. Ford, commanding expanded Ranger companies, rendered a valuable service, but the problem was too great. The voters, in 1859, blamed Governor Runnels, who was vanquished by Houston.

Runnels was a delegate to the Secession Convention and the Constitutional Convention of 1866. About five feet, eight inches tall, of medium size, Runnels had "a florid complexion, with light hair and gray eyes." He never married, his fiancee having cancelled the wedding after he had built a home for her near Boston and ordered furniture from the East, which he hauled from Jefferson by ox cart. Runnels, a Mason and a Texas Historical Society founder, died on Christmas Day, 1873.

Hardin Runnels, the sixth governor, served from December 21, 1857 to December 21, 1859.

The Texans Made "Old Sam Jacinto" Governor

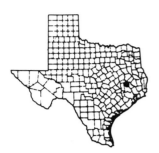

The secession fever was too strong for Sam Houston in 1857. He canvassed Texas by buggy, trying—without success—to avoid his only loss in an election. Marquis James wrote:

> The summer was hot, and he would pull off his shirt and harangue the folk clad in a rumpled linen duster that reached from his neck to his ankles. He stirred the people.... He said things on the stump for which another man would have been shot. This appealed. A legendary hero had come to life—the weatherbeaten figure of "Old Sam Jacinto" himself, with a heart for any fortune and a hand for any fight.

At Brenham, where there was opposition to his speaking in the courthouse, he was eloquent:

> I am not a taxpayer here. I did not contribute to buy a single brick or beam in this building, and have no right to speak here. But if there is a man within the sound of my voice who desires to hear Sam Houston speak and will follow me hence to yonder hillside under the shade of yon spreading live oak, on the soil of Texas, I have a right to speak there because I have watered it with my blood.

Sectional animosities were undiminished when Governor Runnels sought reelection in 1859, but voters were upset about Indian troubles and border raids, and some had begun to fear that secession meant war. Although unwilling to approve of his Unionist views or Know Nothing flirtation, Texans sought the strength and stability of the 66-year-old Houston, who made only one campaign speech, at Nacogdoches. Of Houston's leaving the Senate, the *Washington Evening Star* stated:

> This distinguished man left Washington yesterday afternoon for his home in Texas.... No other public man ever made more, or more sincere, friends here, nor was severance of a gentleman's connection with American public affairs ever more seriously regretted than in his case.

Houston defeated Runnels, 36,227 to 27,500; Edward Clark polled 31,458 votes to Lieutenant Governor Lubbock's 30,325. Because of the legislature's hostility, Houston's inauguration, on December 21, 1859, was held outside. From the capitol's front portico, he told a huge crowd that secession was treason and rebuked extremists on both sides:

> Half the care—half the thought—which has been spent in meeting sectionalism by sectionalism, and bitterness by bitterness, and abolitionism by disunion, would have made this people a happy, united and hopeful nation.

Between Houston's election and inauguration, John Brown raided Harper's Ferry, stirring the fears and hatreds of the secessionists. It was a difficult time. When South Carolina's secession resolutions reached Austin, Sam Maverick wrote:

> What a blessing it is not to have Runnels here now, aggravating the mischief, as he did all the time he was Governor. Old Sam is the right man

Sam Houston, the seventh governor, served from December 21, 1859 until his removal
by the Secession Convention on March 16, 1861.

for this delicate occasion; for S. C. would be fool enough to go out of the Union, if only she had 3 or 4 states to go with her.

When representatives of the seceded states of South Carolina, Mississippi, Alabama, Georgia, Florida, and Louisiana met at Montgomery, Alabama, to form the Confederate States of America, secessionists petitioned for a session of the Texas legislature. Houston stalled until after O. M. Roberts and others had called the Secession Convention. To the legislature, on January 21, 1861, Houston stated that Lincoln's election, while unfortunate, did not justify secession and suggested a convention to examine ways to protect the Southern states while remaining in the Union.

When the convention submitted the secession ordinance to the voters, Houston took to the stump to argue against disunion. Lubbock noted that:

> As an original question, secession, perhaps, would have failed to carry in Texas; but, six leading cotton States had already resorted to an exercise of the right, banded themselves together in a new confederation, and formed a new government. Texas was apparently confronted with the alternatives of becoming a party to the new compact, remaining in the Union, or resuming her sovereignty as a separate republic. Had she desired to desert her sister States of the South in this hour of need and peril (which she did not) and resume her former status as a republic, it was realized that she could not preserve a neutral attitude and maintain herself in that condition. The idea of remaining in the Union, and thereby arraying herself with the avowed enemies of the South, was not to be thought of. The course that was adopted was the only one that was open to her.
>
> Nor was she withheld from it by sentimental considerations. The Northern States generally sympathized with our Mexican enemies in our struggle for independence and opposed our admission into the Union, Massachusetts going so far (by legislative resolution) as to declare the annexation of Texas, ipso facto, a dissolution of the Union. Our people really preferred to fight Massachusetts rather than Louisiana, if fighting should become necessary.

The voters—44,317 to 13,020—approved the ordinance of secession on February 23, 1861. The convention then made Texas part of the Confederacy. When Governor Houston refused to swear allegiance to the new federation, his office was declared vacant. Edward Clark succeeded Sam Houston as governor by taking the required oath.

This old tintype was one of the last likenesses made of Sam Houston.

Clark's Father Was Governor of Georgia

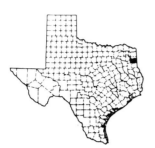

The Secession Convention met on January 28, 1861, with O. M. Roberts presiding. By a vote of 166 to 7 an ordinance was passed dissolving the ties binding Texas to the United States. Representatives to the Confederacy were named, an election was called on the question of secession, and the convention recessed until March 2, the anniversary of Texas' independence from Mexico and Sam Houston's birthday. A popular vote having sustained the secession ordinance, on March 5 the convention united Texas with the Confederacy and ordered state officials to pledge their fidelity to the Confederate States of America. Governor Houston having refused, his office was declared vacant, and Lieutenant Governor Edward Clark became the state's chief executive on March 16.

Llerena Friend, in her fine book on Houston, quoted Presbyterian minister William Baker on this dramatic time:

> As I look back into the darkness of those days, the central figure of them all is that of the old governor sitting in his chair in the basement of the capitol...sorrowfully meditating what it were best to do.... The officers of the gathering upstairs summoned the old man three times to come forward and take the oath of allegiance...to the Confederacy. I remember as yesterday the call thrice repeated—"Sam Houston! Sam Houston! Sam Houston!" but the man sat silent, immovable, in his chair below, whittling steadily on.

And John Kennedy, in *Profiles in Courage* wrote, with a surprising degree of animosity toward Clark:

> The rumbling and contemptuous voices began again. The office of Governor of Texas, Confederate States of America, was declared to be officially vacant; and Lt. Governor Edward Clark, "an insignificant creature, contemptible, spry and pert" stepped up to take the oath. (A close personal and political friend elected on Houston's ticket, Clark would later enter the executive office to demand the archives of the state, only to have his former mentor wheel slowly in his chair to face him with the grandly scornful question: "And what is your name, sir?")

Edward Clark was born on April 1, 1815, in Georgia. He settled in Harrison County, Texas, in 1842, and served in the annexation convention. As a member of J. Pinckney Henderson's staff, he took part in the battle of Monterrey. A member of the first and second legislatures, and secretary of state from 1853 to 1857, Clark was elected lieutenant governor on Houston's independent ticket. His mother, in response to congratulations upon her son's succeeding Houston, answered, "It is natural to have governors in my family. The dress I have on now was worn at my father's inaugural ball in Georgia, later at my husband's inaugural ball in the same state,..." In 1861 Francis Lubbock beat him by a mere 124 votes. Clark raised the 14th Texas Infantry Regiment and was wounded at Pleasant Hill. Brigadier General Clark fled to Mexico at the close of the war. He was practicing law in Marshall at the time of his death, May 4, 1880.

Edward Clark, the eighth governor, succeeded the deposed Sam Houston on March 16, 1861 and served until November 7, 1861.

Francis Lubbock Met the Marquis de Lafayette

Francis Richard Lubbock was a small boy when the Marquis de Lafayette visited South Carolina. Lubbock remembered that the old hero's boat arrived after dark. "A procession was formed to receive our distinguished guest. I was in the line, carrying a sperm candle in each hand. . . . I had the honor of being presented to the illustrious general. . . ." Lubbock lived into the twentieth century. He spent 63 of his 89 years in public office, which enabled him to author a valuable political memoir, *Six Decades in Texas.*

Lubbock was born October 16, 1815, at Beaufort, South Carolina. After holding several man-sized jobs in childhood, he became a druggist in New Orleans. His 17-year-old brother, Tom—after whom the City of Lubbock is named—came to Texas with the New Orleans Greys, and took part in the seige of Bexar. In October, 1836, Francis Lubbock set out to find his brother, bringing a stock of groceries to sell in Texas. He sold the first barrel of flour and first sack of coffee in Houston, nearly became the first mayor, and boasted that "though I did not accompany Columbus when he discovered America. . .I certainly was in at the discovery of Houston. . . ." His two-room house there had no windows. "When air and light were wanted, a board was knocked off. A few rough boards were laid down for the floor, not extending under the bed." (President Houston's mansion was a "small rough log cabin about twelve by sixteen feet, with probably a small shed attached.") To provide a residence for the executive, the Republic purchased, for $6,000, another house owned by Lubbock in Houston.

To succeed Comptroller E. M. Pease, Houston appointed the 22-year-old Lubbock, who wrote after half a century, "In truth, society in Houston at that early day, mixed though it was with some rough characters, and without the sheen of later finery, was just glorious; and I was young. I wonder if I am yet old."

When Lamar became president, Lubbock farmed the place where Santa Anna was captured after the battle of San Jacinto. In 1841 he was elected district clerk of Harris County, and after a few years he bought a ranch near Harrisburg. Patrick Jack urged him, "Do not go into it; the business is not respectable." Lubbock answered, "I believe, judge, I will go into the business to give it respectability."

A slave named Willis asked that Lubbock buy him, since his owner had no other slaves, and he was tired of being the only one "in the cornfield." Lubbock purchased Willis, who was very soft-hearted; once he roped a bear and choked it to death. Close to tears whenever he told the story, Willis vowed never to kill another bear, "for dere is human in 'em sure; it begged and moaned just like a human." When Willis wanted to be free, Lubbock "sold him his freedom, he paying a portion of the money," and when Willis decided to buy his wife and children from their owner, Lubbock guaranteed the unpaid balance. After emancipation Willis still owed part of his own purchase price, and Lubbock had to pay the balance outstanding on Willis' family.

Lubbock hated dogs. Once when he came home from a campaign trip he was attacked by a dog, which he learned belonged to his slave, Louis. Lubbock stated that he would have killed the dog if he had had a gun when he got bit. Louis answered,

Francis Lubbock, the ninth governor, was the second Confederate chief magistrate. His term was November 7, 1861 to November 5, 1863.

"Massa Frank, you can't blame the dog. . . . You ain't home enough dese days for the dogs to know you."

In 1857 Democratic nominees H. R. Runnels—for governor—and Lubbock—lieutenant governor—prevailed over independents Sam Houston and Jesse Grimes. Lubbock canvassed nearly 100 counties and had occasion to become close friends with Congressman John Reagan and study his speaking techniques. He was amazed when, at Jefferson, on the speakers' platform and before a large crowd, Reagan and his opponent became so angry they drew their six shooters and aimed them at each other. Two years later Houston and Edward Clark unseated Runnels and Lubbock. (Although sometimes politically opposed, Houston and Lubbock were good friends.)

Lincoln's election convinced Lubbock that Texas should leave the Union. The Democrats split. The Constitutional Union party was formed in an effort to hold the nation together, and John Bell, of Tennessee, was nominated for president; Colonel A. B. Norton, a Texas delegate to that convention, there to urge Sam Houston's nomination, had pledged a dozen years before not to shave or get a haircut until Henry Clay was President. (Clay was long since dead, but apparently Norton was keeping his vow.) Texas seceded, and Houston, refusing to take an oath to the Confederacy, was succeeded by Edward Clark.

In 1861 Lubbock defeated Clark by 124 out of some 56,000 votes cast. Before taking office he went to Richmond to talk to Confederate officials. On the way home his boat passed a steamer carrying his brother, Lieutenant Colonel Tom Lubbock, of Terry's Texas Rangers. "We recognized each other and signaled a farewell, I going to Texas to my duties as governor, and he, as a soldier, to meet the invaders at the threshold of our Southland. That was our last greeting on earth." Tom Lubbock died soon after taking command of the regiment.

At the same time more men were needed for Indian defense, Texas was having to fill Confederate troop levies. By the end of Lubbock's term, about 60,000 Texans had departed for the fighting in the east. Lubbock called a special session of the legislature to consider the effects of Lincoln's proclamation "declaring all slaves within the Confederate lines free, and inviting them to servile insurrection by advising them to commit no more violence than was necessary to assist and secure their freedom." A law was passed defining the crime of inciting slaves to rebellion.

Lubbock did not seek reelection. He surprised everyone at the November 6, 1863, inaugural ball of Governor Pendleton Murrah by appearing in uniform as a Confederate lieutenant colonel. In the following August, Lubbock joined the staff of Jefferson Davis; he and Postmaster General John Reagan were in the party as the Confederate president fled south after the evacuation of Richmond. Near Irvinsville, Georgia, just before dawn on May 10, 1865, they were captured by Federals. (Lubbock wrote, "I wish here. . .to emphatically brand as false the statement that Mr. Davis was disguised in female apparel.") During the next two years Davis was confined at Fortress Monroe. Reagan and Vice President Alexander Stephens were incarcerated at Fort Warren, in Boston harbor. Lubbock and General Joe Wheeler were imprisoned at Fort Delaware.

Lubbock's cell, 12 x 14 feet, had three barred windows overlooking a moat. "There was no chair, or bed, or blanket, to rest upon, or indeed any article of furniture. . .and there was no light except that furnished by the lamp in the hall. I used my saddle-bags for a pillow, and my Mexican blanket, which I had kept them from robbing me of, to sleep upon." Lubbock was a member of Holland Lodge, at Houston; his treatment improved when the prison commandant discovered he was a Mason. After about six months of solitary confinement he was released. He got home to Houston on December 16, 1865.

Lubbock served as state treasurer from 1879 to 1891. His prominence in Texas government for so many years made him a near-legend. Speaking at a Daughters of the Republic event in Galveston, in 1894, Lubbock told veterans of the Texas revolution:

> A great many people think I was in the battle of San Jacinto. . . . I am sorry, now, that I was not in that battle; for, if I had been, my Texas record would now be complete. And, really, if I had known how few of you would have been killed, I would most certainly have been there.

Francis Lubbock died on June 22, 1905, and was buried in the State Cemetery. He married Adele Baron, his "Creole wife," when she was sixteen and he was nineteen. After her death he married Mrs. Sarah Porter. In 1903—68 years after the first wedding—Lue Scott became his third wife.

Judge Kittrell wrote that:

> Governor Lubbock was not a big man, either physically or intellectually, but he was an absolutely honest man and was a bright, catchy and amusing speaker on the stump, but not a reasoner or deep man mentally . . . .He swore like a trooper, but. . . . He foresook that habit a number of years before he died, and joined the Presbyterian Church . Frank Lubbock carried the baby daughter of Jefferson Davis, later known as "The Daughter of the Confederacy" in his arms to visit her father when he was a prisoner at Fortress Monroe.

Confederate Texas Collapsed Around Murrah

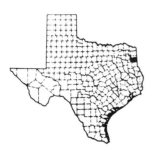

Pendleton Murrah, born in South Carolina in 1824, was orphaned in infancy. (Some sources say he was illegitimate, Murrah was the name of his mother, and his birth occurred in Alabama.) He attended the University of Alabama, graduated from Brown University, and practiced law at Marshall, Texas. He was elected to the legislature in 1857.

As the Democratic congressional nominee, Murrah tried to demolish the Know Nothing party as well as to defeat its candidate. During a speech at Marshall, a member of his audience arose, declared that he had been insulted, and urged every Know Nothing present to follow him out of the hall. To Murrah's dismay almost everyone departed; he was not elected.

There was no Democratic convention in 1863. Murrah won the governorship by polling 17,511 votes to T. J. Chambers' 12,455. Kittrell described Murrah as "a gentleman of culture and ability, an able lawyer. . .a man of modest and gentle demeanor and of rather frail physique." He and Lieutenant Governor Fletcher Stockdale were inaugurated in November. His sixteen months were difficult. He was dying of tuberculosis, the war was going badly, and the impoverished state and the Confederacy were quarreling over Texas' scanty resources.

The Confederate conscript law applied to men between 18 and 54 and the state act made every male between 18 and 50 subject to draft. A Texan was subject to both. He might furnish a substitute or be exempted from one and still be conscripted by the other. Murrah, mainly concerned with having enough troops to guard the ravaged frontier, was in constant conflict with Confederate commanders, who needed those men, too.

The state's only source of ready revenue was cotton, which it bought—giving bonds in payment—and then sold in Mexico. General Kirby Smith, failing to receive adequate support from the Confederacy, began impressing cotton. Farmers were reluctant to accept Confederate certificates, so the state got most of the cotton; the result was that the Army was left in poor financial condition for a winter campaign. Murrah denied that cotton was subject to Confederate impressment, and General Smith retaliated by refusing to allow shipments of the state's cotton across the border. Finally, in July, 1864, Murrah and Smith met in Waller County, and the general agreed to protect the state's cotton in return for the governor's request that farmers sell the rest of their crop to the Army.

The Army requisitioned slaves to build fortifications. It impressed cattle, some of which were not used to feed troops but were sold in Mexico. In late 1864 the Texas legislature declared the impressment of beef unlawful.

On May 9, 1865, at Marshall, General Kirby Smith consulted the governors of Louisiana, Texas, Missouri, and Arkansas. Since he was out of touch with Confederate officials he asked their advice on whether he should surrender. Murrah, too ill to attend, had sent Guy Bryan. The terms of surrender suggested on May 13 included provisions for: the men to be paroled, no one to be prosecuted, and soldiers

Pendleton Murrah was the tenth governor. His term began on November 5, 1863 and ended with the fall of Confederate Texas on June 17, 1865. He had departed for Mexico in the preceding month.

and civilians to be allowed to leave the state. In the meantime the Army was melting. On June 2, General Smith surrendered on a Federal warship at Galveston. John Henry Brown wrote:

> Texas was again in a state of chaos. Governor Murrah called in vain upon the State officers to protect public property, and, on the same day, he performed the ceremony of ordering, by proclamation, a re-assembling of the legislature. . . .

Among those who fled to Mexico were generals Magruder and Smith. The Yankees had imprisoned Governor Letcher, of Virginia, Governor Moore, of Alabama, and others, so Murrah, broken in health, fortune, and spirits, left Texas. He died in Monterrey that August. General Joe Shelby wrote, "He knew death was near to him, yet he put on his old gray uniform, mounted his old war horse, and rode away, dying in Mexico."

Pendleton Murrah's administration was a tragic one. The suicide of a young relative in the Governor's Mansion has long provided a ghost story for the official residence. A fire in the mansion caused Mrs. Murrah to reveal a personal misfortune of longer standing. Sue Ellen Taylor and Pendleton Murrah had had a big wedding in Marshall at her father's house; she was not yet sixteen years old. After the ceremony she went upstairs to wait for him. The guests and the preacher left, and Murrah sat downstairs all night expecting her to come to him. The following morning, Murrah—his pride damaged, apparently for life—took his bride away to their new home. During all the following years the marriage was never consummated. Mrs. Murrah, upset over having to flee the burning mansion, and shocked by his calling her "my dear" in the emergency—the first affectionate words she had heard from him in fourteen years—confided her plight to a neighbor who could not wait to share that confidence with the world. Murrah left her behind when he departed Texas. She died in Tyler in 1868.

Lieutenant Governor Fletcher Stockdale was Texas' chief executive from May to July, 1865. He was a Kentuckian, born about 1823. In addition to his law practice and political activities, he was interested in railroads. His first wife was Mrs. Elizabeth Pryor Bankhead Lytle. After her death he married Elizabeth Schleicher, 17 years old, and they had three children. He died in Cuero in February, 1890.

Lieutenant Governor Fletcher Stockdale took charge after Murrah left for Mexico in May, 1865.

Abraham Lincoln Made Hamilton Governor

Andrew Jackson Hamilton, born January 28, 1815, in Alabama, was largely self-educated. He married Mary Jane Bowen, the daughter of his law partner, and they settled at La Grange, Texas, in 1847. His practice flourished. Governor Bell appointed him attorney general, in 1849, and he moved to the frontier town of Austin.

As a Travis County legislator, Hamilton voted for Senator Sam Houston's reelection in 1853. For a short time he was a Know-Nothing, but soon looked upon those advocates of nativism and secrecy as "the Doodlebugs of America." As an independent, Hamilton was elected to Congress over Democrat T. N. Waul, in 1859. According to Francis Lubbock, "Hamilton had been a prominent Democrat up to this time. He was a man of ability and a powerful debater, and his defection at this juncture proved a great gain to the Independents." That Congress had great difficulty organizing itself: 44 ballots were necessary to elect a speaker, and for awhile it appeared that Hamilton—called "Colossal Jack" because of his intellect—would be the compromise choice.

As Hamilton tried to get congressional authorization for volunteer units to defend the frontier, opponents asserted that Texans provoked the Indian troubles. To Congressman Stanton's charge that some Indian women had been killed in battle, Hamilton answered,

> I will say to the gentleman from Ohio that if he had a dozen arrows shot at him by a squaw, and she was standing ready to let fly the thirteenth, he would not stop long to consider, but would shoot her down with a ball from his revolver without a shudder. The women are dressed so much like the men that it is difficult to tell one from the other in the hurry and excitement of the battle; and thus it sometimes happened that they have shared the fate of the warriors of the tribe.

Hamilton argued against any right of states to secede and promoted a southern route for the Pacific railroad as a means of showing to the South that northern intentions were good. Elected to the state Senate from Hays, Travis, and Bastrop counties—a district that had opposed secession—Hamilton was not seated because of his refusal to take an oath to the Confederacy. Finally, in 1862, his opposition to secession required him to leave Texas. He wrote: "The last thing I saw on looking back from the schooner's deck to the receding shores of Texas was the little launch full of armed men who had failed to catch me." A mob burned his Austin home.

Hamilton made speeches in New York and Boston. Lincoln appointed him provisional governor of Texas, and he was made brigadier general and ordered to raise two volunteer regiments in Texas. From Brownsville—which had fallen to the Federals in 1863—Hamilton advised Texans to abandon the Confederacy.

In 1865 President Andrew Johnson confirmed Hamilton as provisional governor. He was to keep the peace, organize the government, call a convention to amend the constitution, and reconstruct the state. Hamilton and his family reached Galveston on July 21, 1865. They were met by a friendly reception committee—which included Fletcher Stockdale—in Austin a few days later. Hamilton appointed officers—usually

Andrew Jackson Hamilton, the eleventh governor, from July 21, 1865 to August 9, 1866, held office under a provisional appointment made by the president of the United States.

from among Unionists—and investigated the state's finances. He tried to solve the Indian problem and to halt the general lawlessness which prevailed. He counseled freedmen:

> ...you must not think that freedom means more for you than it does for others. It means for you that you have the right to labor for an honest living; the right to obey the command of God to all men, to earn, in the sweat of their face, their daily bread; the right to work for yourselves and receive the full reward of your labor. This is all that freedom means for any people.

Hamilton asked the president to parole former Confederate postmaster general John Reagan from Fort Warren and intervened in behalf of Mrs. Francis Lubbock, whose husband was also in a northern prison. Reagan and Lubbock had been with Jefferson Davis when he was captured.

When the constitutional convention did not provide negro suffrage and otherwise failed to meet congressional expectations, Hamilton warned the delegates of their folly. (Years earlier a newspaper noted that Hamilton, while speaking, "looked like a lion that had broken loose from its keepers.") After all of the wartime acts of the courts and legislature had been approved, he stated:

> I think the friends of this resolution had in mind certain gentlemen here and there who were receivers under the Confederate state laws. They are high-toned reputable gentlemen. They did seize upon that man's property and sell it. They did use their influence to drive out of the country the friends of the Union. They did seize upon horned cattle and horses and mules and household goods even down to the most necessary and delicate appendages of female apparel, which were described in flaming handbills and sold at public auction. Thus the loyal citizens were robbed, and now because these receivers acted under authority they must be protected, and you imagine this convention is powerful enough to protect them. They will and shall be called to an account.
>
> The Congress of the United States is the one to judge whether you have a republican form of government, and if it determines you have not, you will not, you cannot, be admitted.... They will look at your action in reference to the education of the black man. He shall not vote, but he shall be taxed to educate your children. Do you think they will say that this is republicanism?... You have done nothing but deceive yourselves....

Elections were held in August, 1866. Hamilton could not afford to run for governor, but he campaigned for E. M. Pease, who lost to James Throckmorton. Hamilton did not complete his term as governor; after Throckmorton's election the secretary of state became the chief executive while Hamilton went north to assist opponents of President Johnson's plan of easy reconstruction. Hamilton and Pease were delegates to a Philadelphia convention which tried to prevent the South from being controlled by former Confederates, for they were the ones who had persecuted Unionists for opposing secession.

On August 20, 1866, President Johnson proclaimed the rebellion in Texas at an end and ordered the Army to support Throckmorton's government. Congress did not agree; Texas' newly elected senators and congressmen were refused seats; one source said they were not even allowed in the lobbies of the legislative halls. (The senators were former president David G. Burnet and Oran Roberts, the chairman of the Secession Convention.) The first reconstruction act, in March, 1867, enlarged the power of the Army. Then General Philip Sheridan removed Governor Throckmorton, the justices of the Supreme Court, and others as "impediments to reconstruction." That November, Hamilton was appointed to the Supreme Court by General J. J. Reynolds.

Hamilton was a member of the Constitutional Convention of 1869. When Hamilton ran for governor, General Reynolds insisted upon his assistance in obtaining a seat in the United States Senate; in return Reynolds would back Hamilton in the governor's race. Since Reynolds had no qualifications for the office, Hamilton would not help him, and the general supported E. J. Davis. Reynolds' actions were such that Governor E. M. Pease, who had succeeded Throckmorton, resigned and campaigned for Hamilton. Troops were stationed at the polling places, and the election occupied four days. After a suspicious delay and numerous irregularities, including closing polls in some counties known to be favorable to Hamilton, Reynolds announced that Davis was the victor by some 800 ballots.

When the non-partisan taxpayers' convention met to protest excesses of the Davis regime, Hamilton was a delegate. That meeting was the first in a chain of events that would make Richard Coke governor and restore the Democrats to power. Hamilton told them:

> When I came back here I looked upon the Confederate boys, whom I had known in boyhood, whom I knew had fought for their country and for what they believed to be right, and who could have hung me during the war if they had got hold of me. I say I looked to them for protection and I knew I was safe.... But now...no one feels safe from abuse or exempt from arrest at any time.
>
> I am getting old and am not worth much to myself nor anyone else, and I do not wish to be made a martyr of, but I reckon I can afford it as well as anyone else. Generally, I go home from town, get my dinner, and have my wife scratch my head while I go to sleep, but on election day I shall not. I mean to go to the polls and vote, and then stay in town until dark and I wish to see who will arrest me. I am satisfied there will be trouble on that day—I believe it is premediated. . . .

Hamilton died in Austin on April 10, 1865. Governor Pease eulogized him at the funeral, which was held in the capitol.

James Throckmorton Voted Against Secession

Dr. William Throckmorton came to Fannin County, Texas, in 1841; a few months later he moved to a place northeast of McKinney, near present Melissa; he and his family were the first white residents of Collin County. Dr. Throckmorton died in 1843, when his son, James, was eighteen.

James Webb Throckmorton, born in Sparta, Tennessee, on February 1, 1825, served with a Ranger company until, in 1844, he journeyed to Princeton, Kentucky, to study medicine under his uncle, Dr. James Throckmorton. Returning home to serve in the Mexican War, he was a private in Robert Taylor's company of Walter P. Lane's battalion. Throckmorton was commissioned as a second surgeon but was discharged because of illness in June, 1847.

Throckmorton married Annie Rattan, in 1848, and brought her from Illinois to a log cabin he had built. In addition to their ten children they raised five nephews and nieces. He was practicing medicine but hoped to do something else. Throckmorton told a cousin:

> In boyhood I had a yearning for the farm. I commenced life with my family without a home and without a dollar. I had studied medicine to gratify your grandfather. The profession was exceedingly distasteful to me, but an unrelenting necessity forced me to follow it.

Throckmorton studied law and was admitted to the bar in 1851. He spent five years in the House of Representatives and had been five years a state senator when the Secession Convention was called. He made a number of speeches against disunion, and the people of Collin County chose him as a delegate. Enemies accused him of wanting to separate the northern counties from the rest of the state.

The Secession Convention opened at Austin on January 28, 1861, although Governor Houston had tried to abort it. There were 177 delegates present, and Oran Roberts was the president. The secession ordinance was put to a vote on February 1, Throckmorton's 36th birthday. Houston sat on the platform as the delegates were polled. Only Thomas Hughes, of Williamson County, William Johnson, of Lamar County, Joshua Johnson, of Titus County, and A. P. Shuford, of Wood County, had voted against secession when Throckmorton's name was reached. The hall was quiet as he arose and stated, "In view of the responsibility, in the presence of God and my country—and unawed by the wild spirit of revolution around me, I vote 'no.'" He sat down, then angered by the response from the spectators, Throckmorton jumped to his feet and added, "Mr. President, when the rabble hiss, well may patriots tremble." Throckmorton's law partner explained that:

> A single person in the gallery, almost directly over the seat of Throckmorton, hissed in the manner of theatrical loafers. The response was so prompt and so apropos that the whole convention rapturously squelched the screech of the unknown disturber of the solemn scene.

At the conclusion the vote stood 166 to 7. (Near the end of the roll, L. H. Williams and George Wright, both of Lamar County, had voted against secession.)

The twelfth governor, James Throckmorton, took office August 9, 1866 and was removed by General Sheridan on August 8, 1867.

Throckmorton stumped his district. Collin County was persuaded but the statewide count was three to one for disunion. Although Throckmorton had resisted secession, he promised to fight for Texas if war came. He and David Culberson—whose son, Charles, would later be governor—were among those who counseled Sam Houston after Lincoln offered military assistance in holding onto the governor's office. Houston had declined the offer, knowing his acceptance would precipitate violence.

In spite of illness Throckmorton was on active duty as a Confederate officer from the beginning of the war until November, 1863. Then, as a brigadier general, he commanded Texas troops on frontier duty. At the close of the war he was a state senator. Presiding over the Constitutional Convention of 1866, in Austin, Throckmorton advised the delegates: "Let us by our actions strengthen the hand of the executive of the nation, and by a ready and willing compliance with his suggestion show our national brethren that we are in good faith disposed to renew our allegiance to the general government."

In the following election the constitution was approved. Throckmorton, running for governor, received 49,277 votes to 12,168 cast for E. M. Pease. As he took office, on August 9, 1866, the frontier people were desperate. Before the war the U.S. Army had afforded some protection; later Confederate and state troops helped, although the settlements receded a hundred miles. Now they were completely exposed. Throckmorton wanted troops stationed on the frontier, but the administration at Washington kept the 4,000 soldiers in the interior to guard against possible disloyalty. Legislative attempts to raise a volunteer battalion for Indian defense were thwarted by the occupation forces.

As congressional reconstruction was implemented—the act of March 2, 1867, imposed military law upon the former Confederacy—General Philip Sheridan, from New Orleans, on March 19, declared that existing governments in Texas and Louisiana could be abolished. He did not trust Throckmorton, who admitted denouncing Sheridan to correspondents in Washington. "In one of my letters I said that the great misfortune the South labored under was being cursed by military satraps who had not the sense to appreciate the condition of the country, and whose hearts never had a patriotic pulsation." General Griffin complained that the governor was slow to punish offenses against blacks and Unionists and urged his removal. Throckmorton had called Griffin "a dog, mangy and full of fleas, and as mean as the meanest radical in Texas, and that is saying as mean a thing of a man as can be said."

Throckmorton had considered resigning, but he worried about what the generals might do. He believed the military had no authority to oust him or name a successor but knew that Sheridan would do both. On April 29, he was "almost ready to give up the ghost. Almost every hour brings new troubles from the military." The second supplementary reconstruction act, on July 19, gave the generals power to remove civil officers and, on July 30, Sheridan declared Throckmorton to be

> an impediment to reconstruction of the State under the law. He is therefore removed from that office. E. M. Pease is hereby appointed governor of Texas in place of J. W. Throckmorton, removed. He will be obeyed and respected accordingly.

Andrew Johnson, when asked if Throckmorton had tried to thwart Sheridan, said, "No, sir, the records prove the reverse. The governor of Texas placed the whole civil machinery of his state at the disposal of the military power, and aided it in every way possible. . . ." After four terms in Congress, Throckmorton died in McKinney on April 21, 1894.

Gov. J. W. Throckmorton

Throckmorton practiced medicine before he became an attorney and entered politics.

A Yankee General Made Pease Governor Again

Debate on the Kansas-Nebraska Act injected new life into the slavery controversy, and the birth of the new Republican party made Southerners increasingly apprehensive. In 1857 E. M. Pease warned that Republican attacks on slavery were driving the sections further apart. Two years later the question of reopening the African slave trade was raised in the Democratic State Convention. Knowing that advocacy of renewed slave importations was disastrous, Pease broke with the party, although he still considered himself a Democrat. He believed the slave states could best protect themselves by remaining in the Union. He deplored the departure of the first six states, fought the secession of Texas, and objected to the state's joinder to the Confederacy. The convention had no authority to make such a commitment, he said, and therefore Texas was not legally one of the Confederate States.

Pease did not participate in public affairs, nor did he practice law during the war. Because of his aloofness, he retained the confidence of all. He became Andrew J. Hamilton's trusted advisor at a very difficult time; most state officials had fled, and everything pertaining to the government was in confusion.

In the election to adopt the new constitution and elect a governor, James W. Throckmorton defeated Pease, who spent the next two years in Washington. General Sheridan, after removing Throckmorton, appointed Pease to be provisional governor. He was to reorganize the government so that Texas could be readmitted to the Union. Several officials were removed because General Griffin and Pease considered them uncooperative; their replacements were not always accepted by the citizenry, and some offices remained vacant for lack of men willing to serve.

Pease's belief that Texas laws were valid unless unconstitutional or revoked by military orders caused trouble with the radical Republicans. A breach was developing in which Pease's friend, A. J. Hamilton, was opposed by his brother, Morgan Hamilton, and the radicals. Problems increased when General Winfield Scott Hancock succeeded Sheridan and General Griffin died. Hancock's policy of intervening in state affairs only in case of armed resistance left Pease without the support he needed. Since he ruled by order of Congress and the Army and against the will of most Texans—who had elected Throckmorton governor—his abandonment by the Army was serious. Civil officers could not always enforce the law because of lack of popular support. Grand juries would not indict, petit juries would not convict, and lawlessness was epidemic; therefore, Pease believed a few trials by military commission would be beneficial, but Hancock did not agree. Because the prison had been losing money, it was leased for a ten-year term, but the lessee soon defaulted.

In December, 1867, Hancock called for the election of delegates to a constitutional convention which met the following June. Pease reminded the convention that the new document had to be acceptable to Congress, which would require that former slaves be voters and that participants in the war be disfranchised; however, that deprivation of voting was only temporary, he was certain. The new constitution would have to nullify laws which had aided the rebellion and those discriminating against

Elisha Pease, the thirteenth governor, was appointed by General Sheridan on August 8, 1867. He resigned, September 30, 1869, because of General Reynolds' interference in the governor's election, and Texas had no chief executive for three months.

freedmen. All debts incurred in behalf of the Confederacy had to be repudiated. None of these requirements were popular, and it required a brave man to state them. Pease risked everything in following his conviction that Texas was best served by accepting the requirements of the congressional radicals. Once readmitted, the state could return to normal.

Hoping to continue reconstruction, the convention's radical faction, led by E. J. Davis, tried to frustrate adoption of any constitution. In the ratification election Pease favored the gubernatorial candidacy of A. J. Hamilton. Unfortunately, General J. J. Reynolds, the state commander, wanted Davis to win. Pease resigned, on September 30, 1869, because of Reynolds' interference in the election. There was no governor until Reynolds finally announced, several weeks later, that Davis had won. Francis Lubbock wrote:

> In the preliminary steps of congressional reconstruction, intelligence and worth were proscribed and a premium put on ignorance and barbarism. All discriminations were against the white race. The negroes voted en masse, and enough whites were disfranchised to ensure a Republican majority in the convention. At the election for State officers under the new Constitution E. J. Davis was counted in for Governor by the exclusion of several Democratic counties that gave majorities for A. J. Hamilton.

Abuses of the Davis administration provoked a severe reaction. Three former governors, Hamilton, Throckmorton, and Pease, at a July, 1870, meeting called by them, condemned the Davis administration and drafted a petition to Congress for a republican form of government. In the next year Pease presided over the taxpayer's convention that marked the beginning of Democratic recovery. Its sessions—and the 1872 amnesty allowing disfranchised Democrats to vote—resulted in Richard Coke's election. Pease was a delegate to the Cincinnati convention at which liberal Republicans nominated Horace Greeley for president.

Pease had earned very little during his time in public life. Except for two years as the customs collector at Galveston, after resigning the governorship he lived at Austin. He handled many important lawsuits, for colleagues believed he knew in detail every pre-Civil War statute. In 1877, Pease, John Breckenridge, and R. T. Breckenridge organized the First National Bank of Austin. A Mason and member of St. David's Episcopal Church, Pease died at Lampasas, where he had gone for a rest, on August 26, 1883.

E. M. Pease moved to Woodlawn at the close of his first administration. A hundred years later Governor Allan Shivers purchased the mansion as his own term expired.

E. J. Davis Was the Reconstruction Governor

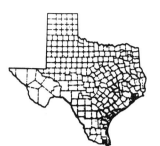

When the Republicans who ruled Texas began quarreling among themselves, E. J. Davis was the leader of the radicals. The breach became apparent over validity of the state's actions during the war. In the Constitutional Convention of 1868 the Davis group contended that every statute enacted during the war was void. The moderates, led by A. J. Hamilton and E. M. Pease, held them invalid only when they conflicted with the national constitution and statutes. Another divisive argument concerned the radicals' wish to disfranchise everyone who had aided the Confederacy.

Hamilton was defeated for the governorship by Davis, who was assisted by the state's commander. General Reynolds, suggesting that his West Point friendship with President Grant would be advantageous to Texas, wanted to be a United States Senator. Hamilton opposed him; Reynolds was not a Texan and was not qualified for the office. Reynolds told Grant that Hamilton's election would start a Confederate revival; his manipulations caused Governor Pease to resign and campaign for Hamilton.

Reynolds ordered new voter registration lists; these were compiled mainly by soldiers and Davis men who disfranchised many qualified voters. Troops stationed at the polls probably kept some Democrats away. Only about half of the 78,648 registered whites voted, while a much larger percentage of the 56,905 freedmen participated. The four-day election began November 30, 1869, with those who prepared the registration lists serving as election officers. More than a month passed before Reynolds, on January 8, 1870, appointed Davis as provisional governor and J. W. Flanagan as lieutenant governor. The Army later reported that Davis had received 39,901 votes, Hamilton 39,092, and the Democrat Stuart 380.

The election's many irregularities included the failure to open the polls in Navarro County, which leaned toward Hamilton and had about 1,000 voters; the presiding official—a non-resident of the county—ran off with the voter list. Milam County polling places were ordered closed, and no ballots were counted. Hill County ballots were taken into another jurisdiction and tabulated by one official, who reported a Davis majority. El Paso County reported 339 votes for Davis and 122 for Hamilton, although 277 men swore that they had voted for Hamilton. Pease asked the President to investigate the election, but nothing came of it. This stormy beginning foreshadowed the most turbulent administration of any Texas governor.

Born October 2, 1827, in St. Augustine, Florida, Edmund Jackson Davis, about 1848, came with his family to Galveston, where his father died. He read law at Corpus Christi and was a deputy customs collector at Laredo. In 1853 he became the district attorney at Brownsville and was a district judge when he married Anne Britton at Corpus Christi, in 1859. When Texas seceded he fled to Mexico; there he raised a Federal cavalry regiment of Texans. Some Confederates captured him at Matamoras, but he was released after the Mexicans protested. At the close of the war he was a brigadier general. As leader of the radicals in the 1866 convention, Davis wanted Texas divided into three parts. Apparently he believed the radicals could control at least one of the new states.

Edmund J. Davis, the fourteenth governor, served from January 8, 1870 to January 15, 1874.

When General Reynolds, in 1870, convened the new officials as the provisional government, the legislature ratified the 14th and 15th amendments and chose as United States senators Morgan C. Hamilton, the radical brother of moderate A. J. Hamilton, and J. W. Flanagan, the recently-elected lieutenant governor. (Reynolds had realized he stood no chance of election to the Senate.) On March 30, 1870, Grant signed the bill readmitting Texas, and a few days later Reynolds turned over the government to the civil officers.

Davis, in his April 28 inaugural address, explained the need for a state police force. That body would cause much of the trouble that plagued Texas in the next few years. Its stormy history peaked in 1871 when members murdered some citizens. Texans feared the state police, and their presence at the polls inhibited elections. In late 1872 the chief, James Davidson, ran away to Belgium with $34,000 in state funds, and a few months later, after Democrats attained a legislative majority, the law establishing the police force was repealed over Davis' veto. Denton citizens celebrated by firing anvils.

Davis had great power because of the many offices that were his to fill by appointment: district attorneys, county treasurers, clerks, surveyors, mayors, aldermen, and others. John Henry Brown, after an extensive listing, stated: "This is by no means all of the Governor's power and patronage, but here are nine thousand five hundred and twenty-eight persons appointed, directly or indirectly, by him to places of trust, honor, or profit, or all combined."

In May, 1870, legislators unconstitutionally extended their terms one year by declaring that no election could be held until November, 1872, because the people were not yet ready for political strife. The action alienated Senator Morgan Hamilton from the radicals.

Efforts to unseat Davis began in 1871 when E. M. Pease and others called a taxpayers' convention to consider the administration's burdensome taxation and reckless spending. Ninety-four counties sent delegates—Democrats and moderate Republicans—to Austin that September. Major George B. Erath, of Waco, opened the convention; Pease was the permanent chairman. The delegates resolved to ask congressional assistance if the election cancellation were not reversed. By then the radicals had realized the necessity of an election because congressional terms were expiring; in the special election of October, 1871, despite assignment of state police and militia to the polls, all four Democratic congressional candidates won. In 1872 the Democrats captured a majority of the seats in the legislature. The nominee of their national party, Horace Greeley, defeated President Grant in Texas.

A major controversy concerned whether Davis' term was four years from January 17, 1870, when he became provisional governor, or four years from his April 28, 1870, inaugural. Anti-radical majorities in the legislature considered impeaching Davis in 1873 but were restrained by the possibility of federal interference. Even after Richard Coke defeated Davis, in December, 1873, the radicals thought they had another chance; a criminal prosecution offered the possibility of invalidating the whole election.

Jose Rodriguez, of Houston, had been arrested for voting twice, and an application for a writ of habeas corpus was made to the Supreme Court of Texas on the ground that the election law was unconstitutional. The statute under attack, passed by Democrats, permitted voting in the precincts and limited the election to one day. The changes made it harder to control elections, for under the old law the radicals had to watch only one polling place, at the county seat. Davis objected but signed the bill into law.

In *Ex Parte Rodriguez*—"the semi-colon case"—the Supreme Court had to decide whether voting could be confined to one day, for the constitution provided that:

> All elections for State, District and County offices shall be held at the county seats of the several counties, until otherwise provided by law; and the polls shall be opened four days, from 8 o'clock a.m., until 4 o'clock p.m. of each day.

The radicals admitted that the first clause permitted the legislature to establish polls outside the county seat, but they argued the clause following the semi-colon was not subject to change; and, therefore, elections had to extend over four days. The Supreme Court agreed that the semi-colon was just such a barrier, that permission given in the first clause for the legislature to make changes did not apply to the second clause. The court invalidated the election held under the statute. The decision would have caused much confusion, since hundreds of officials had been chosen in that election. Fortunately, Texans ignored "the semi-colon case," and Coke and the others elected under the statute took office. Grant refused Davis' request for help, saying:

> The act of the legislature of Texas providing for the recent election having received your approval, and both political parties having made nominations, and having conducted a political campaign under its provisions, would it not be prudent as well as right, to yield to the verdict of the people as expressed by their ballots?

Although Davis believed his term did not end until April, he left office, under protest, in January, 1874. With his departure, reconstruction in Texas was finally over.

Davis opened a law office in Austin. He was the Republican candidate for governor in 1880 and was badly beaten by O. M. Roberts. He died February 7, 1883, not long after losing a race for Congress, and was buried in the State Cemetery.

Richard Coke Threw the Rascals Out

Richard Coke, born March 13, 1829, in Williamsburg, Virginia, graduated from the College of William and Mary and was admitted to the bar before moving to Waco in 1850. Governor Runnels appointed him to the commission which negotiated removal of the Brazos Reservation Indians to land north of Red River. At the age of 23 he married the fifteen-year-old Mary Horne at Waco. (Of their four children, Jack died while attending Baylor and the other son, Richard, did not attain his 29th birthday. Two daughters had died as children.)

Coke served in the Secession Convention. At the beginning of hostilities he joined the Army as a private. He became a company commander in the 15th Texas Regiment and served until the end of the war. A district judge by appointment of Governor Hamilton, in 1866 he was elected to the Supreme Court, but he was one of the "impediments to reconstruction" removed by General Sheridan.

Francis Lubbock described E. J. Davis' reconstruction government as "the most intolerable ever known in Texas. Venality and tyranny were rampant, all the safeguards of liberty were overthrown, the people harassed by a negro police, and property threatened finally with confiscation." Exasperated Texans from both parties and 94 counties came together in the September, 1871, taxpayers' convention, and their indictment of the Davis regime began the recovery of the government by the people. The delegates included governors Pease, Throckmorton, and Hamilton and future governor John Ireland. Legislators elected the next year repealed some of the obnoxious laws and began dismantling the reconstruction government.

In 1873 the Democrat Richard Coke overwhelmed Davis, 103,038 ballots to 51,220, and Richard Hubbard won the lieutenant governor's office from Robert H. Taylor. Davis, disinclined to surrender his office, insisted upon remaining until April 28, the fourth anniversary of his inauguration. The public was outraged but not surprised. Davis asked President Grant for help, but the President replied that Davis should yield since the new officials had been elected fairly.

Democratic legislators, on January 12, decided to organize the following morning—the day set by law for them to meet—despite anticipated resistance. The incumbent radical Republicans, calling themselves the true legislature, declared that they would convene the next day. That evening William A. Pitts and H. C. Surghnor, finding the lower part of the capitol occupied by some of Davis' armed militia, managed to get upstairs. They held the House and Senate chambers—by barring the doors—until morning, when the new legislature organized. The old legislature was trying to do business downstairs, but neither House nor Senate could muster a quorum. On the 15th, Davis finally turned over the election returns, which the new legislature canvassed. Coke and Hubbard were then inaugurated.

Because the number of armed men downstairs kept increasing, Coke ordered General Henry McCulloch—who had just been made a deputy sheriff—to prevent conflict between the two factions. Coke feared that violence would provide an excuse for the Army to install another military government.

Davis still refused to acknowledge Coke as governor on January 17, but the

The fifteenth governor, Richard Coke, held office from January 15, 1874 to December 1, 1876.

problem was resolved that day when Grant's attorney general refused Davis' third request; he stated that the President "does not feel warranted in furnishing United States troops to aid you in holding further possession of it and therefore declines to comply with your request." Two days later Coke was in possession of the governor's office, and the legislature thanked Grant for his restraint. Francis Lubbock recalled that morning in January, 1874, which "dawned upon Texas redeemed from radical rule, upon Texas free and at peace for the first time since 1861."

According to Oran Roberts, "Coke's administration entered upon another reconstruction of the State of Texas—a Democratic reconstruction—to restore the operation of the State government...." Of a questionable railroad grant, Coke said:

> On the 5th day of August, 1870, when the legislature, composed for the most part of strangers to the State and people of Texas, chosen at an election when less than one-fourth of the tax-payers were allowed to vote, occupied the halls of the capitol, the agents of the International Railroad Company, by the most fraudulent and corrupt means, procured the enactment of the charter under which they make the claim. The charter grants $10,000 per mile for the construction of a road from Jefferson to Laredo on the Rio Grande, and exemption from taxation for five years....

At the election in which Coke won a second term, the present constitution was adopted. A few days after his inauguration he was elected to the United States Senate; however, Coke remained governor until December, 1876. Kittrell described him as "a tall, ungainly, unpretentious, ungraceful man, who went about without bluster or parade, never seeking the limelight. His home was right here among us in Texas—not in Greece or Rome, yet he was a great intellect—his enemies so conceded...." When he was threatened with violence because of his veto of a railroad bill, former lieutenant governor Fletcher Stockdale and others offered their aid. Coke turned them away, saying:

> If any man puts his foot within the limits of these grounds with the intent to insult me or offer any indignity to my family or myself, I'll be damned if he goes out again until he is carried out feet foremost on a stretcher.

Kittrell wrote, "If the question were put to me, 'who in your judgment would be the ablest man intellectually ever connected with the government of Texas?' I would answer without hesitation, 'Richard Coke.' "

When he was invited to a White House function Senator Coke had a hard time finding a big enough pair of white gloves. He reported:

> My hands looked like a pair of canvassed hams, but I wore 'em. But the gloves weren't the worst of my troubles. It was the trails of the women's dresses. I saw a powerful fine-looking woman bowing to me, and I bowed, and she bowed, and I bowed again. I didn't know who she was, but thought maybe she desired to see me, so I started towards her. When I moved, she moved off, with her back to me. Now do you know what was the matter? I was standing on the trail of her dress, and I'll swear I weren't in fifteen feet of her.

Senator Sam Bell Maxey asked, "Did you get your gloves off safely?" Coke answered, "Hell, I tore 'em off."

After three terms in the Senate, Coke returned to Waco. He died at his plantation on May 14, 1897.

Richard Coke, indicated by the "X", attends a meeting of former Confederates at Robert Lee, in the county named for him. In the background is the partially finished Coke County courthouse.

In Waco's Oakwood Cemetery Governor Coke's statue is flanked by busts of his sons.

Richard Coke stands looking at his friend, Dr. David R. Wallace. The statues were unveiled in 1898, while Wallace, a pioneer in psychiatric medicine in Texas, was still practicing.

Richard Hubbard Weighed 300 Pounds

Because of his ability as a speaker, Richard Bennett Hubbard, "the Demosthenes of Texas," was the state's Centennial Orator at the Philadelphia Exposition, on July 4, 1876, and temporary chairman of the Democratic convention that nominated Grover Cleveland for president. Cleveland, in gratitude for Hubbard's speeches in his behalf, made him the United States Minister to Japan. Hubbard, born November 1, 1832, in Georgia, graduated from Mercer College. After attending the University of Virginia, his law degree was conferred by Harvard University. He was a successful attorney at Tyler, Texas.

Hubbard campaigned against the Know Nothings and helped elect James Buchanan. After two years as United States Attorney, he was elected to the legislature. In the 1860 Democratic convention at Charleston he supported John C. Breckenridge. He raised the 22nd Texas Infantry Regiment and became a Confederate colonel. Hubbard farmed until he was pardoned for participation in the rebellion, then resumed his law practice. A delegate to the 1872 Democratic National Convention, Hubbard campaigned for the nominee, Horace Greeley.

Hubbard ran for lieutenant governor in 1873. He and Richard Coke made a vigorous and effective canvass and—as Oran Roberts put it—"the mass of the people, on the day of the election, rushed to the polls and cast their votes for the redemption of the State from the ignominy and ruin with which it was threatened by the continuance of such Republican rule."

The Davis people hoped to remain in office by the invalidation of the December 2, 1873, election. In a habeas corpus hearing for a petitioner charged with voting twice, it was urged that the election was a nullity. The Supreme Court agreed that the statute violated the constitutional provision that "All elections. . .shall be held at the county-seats of the several counties until otherwise provided by law; and the polls shall be opened for four days, from eight o'clock a.m. until four o'clock p.m. of each day." The questioned election was held on one day in the four precincts of each county. The court held that the semi-colon separated two different requirements: (1) elections were to be at the county seat *unless otherwise provided*, and (2) polls were to be open for four days. Although the legislature could allow polling away from the county seat, the semi-colon was such a complete barrier that the "unless otherwise provided" did not apply to the second clause and would not permit one-day elections. Governor Davis used the "semi-colon case" to try to stay in office. Hubbard, Coke, and the new legislature ignored the decision, avoiding the confusion which would have resulted if new elections had been required for the hundreds of offices voters believed they had just filled.

When Coke resigned to enter the Senate, on December 1, 1876, Hubbard became governor. He was about 5 feet 9 inches tall and weighed 300 pounds. His first marriage was to Eliza Hudson, and after her death he married Janie Roberts, of Tyler. She died in Japan, but her body was brought back to Tyler.

Hubbard was a learned, gentle man. Once he told the attorney general that while

Richard Hubbard became governor on December 1, 1876, when Coke resigned to enter the Senate, and served until January 21, 1879.

he was at home at lunch that day a mother and wife came there pleading for him to commute the death sentence of their son and husband and, "The mother cried, and the wife cried, and damn it, I cried. Oh, it was a fearful time, but I can't pardon the man who committed such a crime." The sentence was carried out.

The legislature did not meet during Hubbard's term—December 1, 1876, to January, 1879. At the Democratic State Convention, in July, 1878, he was the leading candidate but was contested by James W. Throckmorton and W. W. Lang, the head of the state grange. In the balloting Hubbard got a majority each time but he could not muster the 2/3 vote needed for nomination. On the seventh day it was clear that no one could achieve the required support. Oran Roberts was offered as a compromise candidate and was nominated by acclamation.

Hubbard was Minister to Japan from 1885 to 1889. When Kittrell once asked him about Japanese morals he said:

> "A man can have his concubine, but before he enters into that kind of relation, he must, with money, or stocks, or bonds, or other property, insure the comfort of his legitimate family, and that is very just. Then again they have a regulation that he must not keep the concubine in the part of the city where his family lives. . . ." Hubbard then grimaced, his eyes twinkled, and he punched me in the ribs with his thumb and said: "And let me tell you, that is a first-class, sensible kind of arrangement, sure as you are born."

His book, *The United States in the Far East*, was published in 1899. He died on July 12, 1901, at Tyler. The city of Hubbard was named for him.

–Austin-Travis County Collection, Austin Public Library

Hubbard, the sixteenth governor, was a noted orator and became the United States Minister to Japan.

Roberts Was the "Old Alcalde"

Oran Milo Roberts was born July 9, 1815, in South Carolina, the youngest of six children. He was three years old when his family moved to Alabama. Because of his father's early death, Roberts did a man's work in the fields from the age of ten years. He entered the University of Alabama in spite of meager finances and a poor educational background. By the time his degree was conferred, he was the university librarian. He read law, was admitted to practice in 1837, and was the first college graduate elected to the legislature from his county.

In 1841 Roberts moved to San Augustine, Texas. President Houston made him the district attorney, and Governor Henderson appointed him judge of the district. He was teaching law in the University of San Augustine when he became a Supreme Court justice in 1857.

As chairman of the Secession Convention, it was Roberts' duty, on March 4, 1861, to announce that Texas was no longer part of the United States. After raising and leading an infantry regiment, Colonel Roberts resigned his commission to serve as chief justice of the Supreme Court. The legislature elected Roberts and David G. Burnet as senators in 1866, but the Senate refused to seat them because of their Confederate past. Roberts was practicing law in Gilmer when Governor Richard Coke appointed him chief justice again.

In 1878 the Democrats had trouble choosing a nominee. Unable to attain the necessary 2/3 majority, Hubbard still led every ballot. After a week of stalemate the state convention chose Roberts by acclamation. Notified by telegram at Tyler, where he was then farming and practicing law, he told a friend, "Lend me four bits and I will accept the nomination." That November Roberts drew 158,733 votes to Republican A. B. Norton's 23,402 and Greenbacker W. H. Hammon's 55,002. Joseph Sayers was elected lieutenant governor. In his inaugural address Roberts said:

> Standing in this place on the 4th day of March, 1861, as the president of the seceding convention, and acting by their authority, I proclaimed Texas a free and independent state. I did it in good conscience, believing it to be right. I now, with the same good conscience, as the governor of the State, declare Texas to have been in good faith reconstructed. . . . I now believe that the chief effort should be placed upon building up a great State. . . .

Never without his corn cob pipe, before Roberts took the oath of office he handed the pipe to a friend.

Frank Norton, in his fine thesis, noted that "no stronger charge of immorality was ever brought against him than that he occasionally, as a matter of fact, usually, after his day's work was done, took a toddy as he went from his office to the mansion." He was censured for failure to profess religious convictions, the critics usually being preachers who did not approve of the University of Texas. After James A. Garfield was wounded, Ohio's chief executive asked the other governors to set aside a day of prayer for the President's recovery. Only the governor of Texas failed to comply. Accused then of impiety, Roberts answered, "I do not deem it consistent with my position as

Oran Roberts, the seventeenth governor; his term began on January 21, 1879 and ended January 16, 1883.

Governor to issue a proclamation directing religious services, where Church and State, are and ought to be, kept separate in their functions."

Texas still labored under the burdens of the Davis administration, whose large expenditures had raised the bonded debt substantially. Roberts' investigation showed

> that the state had not in thirty years been able to pay current expenses with the revenue collected annually, and that there was then an estimated outstanding debt of three hundred thousand dollars—afterwards found to be four hundred thousand dollars—with no means on hand to pay it. . . .

The legislature imposed several new taxes, all designed to keep the burden off the farmers. The most interesting was the Bell Punch tax. Where liquor was consumed on the premises, a tax of 1/2¢ was to be collected on malt drinks and 2¢ on all others. Every saloon was to purchase a register for malt drinks and one for alcoholic drinks. Each register had a bell which sounded when the crank was turned and a counter showing the number of revolutions of the crank. The bartender was to turn the crank each time a drink was served, and the patron was not to pay until he heard the bell. Collectors assessed taxes monthly according to the figures shown on the registers. It was a complete failure. The *Brenham Banner* said: "The Bell Punch demonstrates the fact that public opinion is superior to the law. Public opinion condemned the Bell Punch at the start."

Roberts' "pay as you go" program reduced the public debt and improved state finances. Through his efforts and his realization of the state's dearth of educated teachers, the Sam Houston State Normal School and Prairie View Normal School were established. He was also responsible for founding the University of Texas. A site committee chose Austin because of 40 acres there that Congress had set aside in 1839. The cornerstone was laid in 1882, and instruction began the next fall. After he left office, Roberts—who was called by the students "the old Alcalde"—and another judge constituted the law faculty.

Dean T. U. Taylor, Roberts' colleague at the university, was surprised once when the old man claimed to have failed in life, saying,

> I was absorbed in law, in public affairs, and I neglected the greatest thing in this world—the education of my children—until it was *too late*. When I realized that. . .they were then too big to go into classes with much smaller children.

One evening, years later, a gray-haired man with a lantern stopped by Taylor's office. After asking his name and learning that the watchman was Roberts' son, Dean Taylor wrote:

> My mind leaped across the intervening thirty years, and I recalled the statement made to me by the old Alcalde as we walked along Nueces Street when, for three times, he muttered the words *too late*. Here was his son, grayhaired, sixty years old, night watchman in the institution that his father in 1881 signed the bill to create.

Kittrell wrote:

> Perhaps no man was ever better known in Texas since the days of Sam Houston than was Oran Milo Roberts, and no man was more deeply entrenched in popular confidence and respect. He was a singular combination of intellect and almost childish simplicity. . . . He was

popular, yet he had none of the arts of the demagogue. . . . He had none of the arts of the orator. It is doubtful if he ever attempted a simile or a metaphor in the course of a public speech in all of his life, but he knew what he meant to say, and said it in clear-cut English, and his patriotism and Spartan integrity, and his unselfish devotion to Texas, gave insight to what he said. Every man who heard him knew there was behind what he said, that which must be behind every speech if it has any weight, or in anywise influences popular action, namely—a man.

Norman G. Kittrell (after whom the town of Normangee was named) was a judge for many years. He considered Roberts' judicial performance superb but was fascinated by his simplicity.

It was almost inconceivable that a man who could write such opinions ...could be at the same time so absolutely simple in speech and action as he was at times. . . . On one occasion I heard him talking about his experiences in the army. . .and he said, "I threw my regiment across the creek;" then he stopped and in perfect seriousness made the following explanation: "Now you understand I didn't take each man up myself and pitch him across the creek." This was not said in the way of a jest, but in seriousness, as if he thought it necessary that he should not be literally understood as having thrown eight hundred or a thousand men across the stream by sheer physical force.

I believe it was Sir Isaac Newton, the wisest of all scientists, who, when asked why he cut two holes in the door of his bedroom, replied that one was for the big cat to come in, and the other for the little cat.

Roberts married Frances Edwards in Alabama. She died in 1883. A few years later he married Mrs. Catherine Border. Governor Roberts died in Austin on May 19, 1898.

Ireland Was "Ox Cart John"

Born on January 21, 1827, John Ireland was one of fourteen children in a very poor Kentucky family. His mother died when he was twelve, and he received only a rudimentary education. As a Hart County deputy sheriff and constable, he read law and was admitted to the bar. In 1853, he moved to Seguin, Texas, where he married Mrs. Matilda Wicks Faircloth. They had one child; after the death of his wife he married Anne Maria Penn, in 1857.

After serving as the mayor of Seguin he was a delegate to the Secession Convention. Enlisting as a private, he was a lieutenant colonel by the time he left the Army to serve on a Confederate court which had criminal jurisdiction over both civilians and military personnel.

Ireland was a member of the Constitutional Convention of 1866, and was one of the district judges removed from office by General Sheridan. He was elected to the Texas House in 1872 and to the Senate two years later. His opposition to railroad subsidies caused opponents to label him "Ox Cart John"; they said wagons and beasts of burden were destined to be Texas' only form of transportation if Ireland had his way, but Ireland's enemies respected him and admitted his sincerity in opposing monopoly and special privilege.

The Democrats, after Governor Roberts refused to run again, nominated John Ireland, in 1882. Edmund Davis presided over the Republican convention that year; the party had barely survived, and delegates did not nominate a candidate. A group which called itself the Independents was led by former lieutenant governor George Washington Jones. Senator Richard Coke said they were disappointed office-seekers pledged to nothing but the occupancy of whatever places they might capture. "Wash" Jones, a former Whig, Know-Nothing, Democrat, and Greenbacker, was surprisingly strong; he received 102,501 votes to Ireland's 150,809. Ireland had not run as well as Roberts, two years earlier. Mrs. Ireland did not approve of dancing and did not attend the inaugural ball. A friend wrote that she would represent Mrs. Ireland in the grand march. The new governor's wife answered, "If you represent me, you will stay at home; that is what I am doing."

The main policy difference between Roberts and Ireland concerned the public lands. The new governor hoped to retain every acre until an advantageous price would be realized, whereas Roberts had wanted a rapid sale. Ireland pointed out that only a fragment remained of the 120 million acres owned by Texas in 1865. A million acres had been set aside for the University of Texas, land had been earmarked to benefit state institutions for the deaf, the insane, the blind, and the orphans, and thirty million acres had been given to the public schools. Proceeds from the sale of those lands went into the institutions' permanent funds. Ireland demanded that minimum prices be set for each parcel and that sales be made on the highest bid.

The two governors also differed on educational expenditures. While Roberts had advocated development of the new state university, Ireland would not risk reductions in public school support to benefit higher education.

Texas' land problems were complicated by a new factor: fencing. The booming

88

John Ireland, the eighteenth governor, served from January 16, 1883 to January 18, 1887.

cattle business was attracting capital from the North and from Europe. Before 1876 East and South Texas were cattle country, but with the retirement of the Plains Indians the cattle business spread west and north. In 1883 four corporations, each with a million dollar capitalization, were chartered at Gainesville. Livestock prices had gone up 500% between 1870 and 1884, making good land and water increasingly valuable.

With the invention of barbed wire it was possible to enclose large areas of open country; cowmen could upgrade herds by selective breeding and keep their pastures and water for the exclusive use of their herds. Barbed wire was first sold in Texas, in 1875, in Gainesville. As fences began to appear, those who had always used the open range were angered. Some, such as Austin's J. L. Driskill—who had 800 animals—owned herds but no land. Their cattle grazed the countryside. Fenced ranges resulted in closed roads; and detours of up to fifty miles were required to reach towns only a short distance away by crow-flight. Barbed wire made farming possible in West Texas, for fences kept cattle out of the fields. The "free grass" men were dismayed by the number of farmers moving in. With fencing, fewer cowboys were needed, and unemployed hands were not above declaring war on fences. The sympathetic *Waco Examiner*, in 1883, published this "Song of the Wire Cutters:"

> Get up your scissors, boys,
> And mount your gamest steeds,
> There's work for us tonight,
> To the prairies we will speed.
>
> What right has bloated capital,
> To fence our prairies fair—
> We'll cut the insolent wires,
> And make music in the air.

Public sentiment often favored the vandals, and sometimes officials were afraid to enforce the laws against them. The Waco paper said the fence cutters were not "communists" but simply believed that one should "Do a wrong to redress a wrong." By one estimate the damage to fences in two years was $20 million. Another stated that losses would exceed $1 million in Brown County alone. The *Austin Statesman*, in 1883, stated that: "Fence cutting prevails in this section to an alarming degree and if not stopped the rope and mob are liable to be resorted to."

A special session of the legislature, called by Ireland in 1884, made wire-cutting a felony. Builders of fences had to provide gates every three miles and were prohibited from enclosing land owned by another. The statute helped end the fence-cutting, and the public approved, for Ireland's reelection vote was 212,234 compared to 150,809 two years before, and Jones' total dropped from 102,501 to 88,540.

Maggie Smith, in her fine study of the Ireland years, observed that Texas, with less than 500 miles of railroad track in 1870, had 7,889 miles in 1887. Much of that track was in new country, where there were few passengers and shippers of freight. Although the companies had received great quantities of land, they were in bad financial shape. At the same time, they were guilty of discriminatory rates, rebates, and other abuses. Despite his reputation, "Ox Cart John" Ireland, not wanting to jeopardize railroad development, approached the problem with caution. He suggested the establishment of a railroad commission, but the legislature did not respond.

Significant educational advances were made during Ireland's tenure. A constitutional amendment authorizing a real system of public education provided for school districts with taxing power. The position of State Superintendent of Education was established and the school laws were revised to provide the stability which encouraged men and women to become teachers. The legislation was based upon a belief in state responsibility for educating the young—a principle that was a long time in gaining acceptance. The scholastic population more than doubled from 1880 to 1886.

The University of Texas opened in September, 1883. Classes met in the temporary capitol pending completion of the Main Building. The university's future was uncertain; in early 1885 it had only 130 students, more than half from Austin. Private colleges did not wish it well, nor did A. & M., which would struggle for survival until Sul Ross took it over. The *Clarksville Northern Standard*'s opinion was not untypical:

> All thoughtful citizens who have comprehension of such a subject know that the attempt to start such an institution in completeness when this was started was absurd. The scholars had not been educated sufficiently or in sufficient number to afford food for such an institution. ...All intelligent people of the State are able. to see now that the University was pushed forward prematurely, for the double purpose of furnishing positions to decayed professionals and to create a tub mill for Austin. It has answered that purpose for the State, which is really discredited by claiming as a State university a mere collegiate institution in which not a single professor has a reputation that would draw a scholar from a distance, or confer credit upon a university proper.

Of the new capitol, begun in Ireland's administration, Lubbock wrote:

> The contractors insisted on using Indiana limestone. Governor Ireland stated emphatically that he would not sign a contract that would permit the building to be erected of foreign stone. . . . The Governor and myself, as members of the board, stood firm and, as a result, the contractors came to our terms and the capitol was built wholly of Texas granite, limestone, and marble. . . .

The second baby born in the Governor's Mansion was that of Ireland's daughter; the child died in infancy. (Temple Houston was the first born there, and Sam Houston Allred was the third.)

After leaving office, Ireland practiced law in Seguin. His attempt at a Senate seat was frustrated by John Reagan. While on a trip to San Antonio, Ireland became ill; he died there on March 15, 1896.

Sul Ross Was "Soldier, Statesman, and Knightly Gentleman"

Lawrence Sullivan Ross, born September 27, 1838, in Bentonsport, Iowa, was brought to Texas before he was a year old. (His father, Shapley Prince Ross, built the first house in Waco.) He attended Baylor, at Independence, and graduated from Wesleyan University at Florence, Alabama, in 1859. During the vacation before his senior year he came home, which was then the Indian reservation administered by his father near Fort Belknap. With 135 Brazos Agency Indians Sul Ross joined Major Earl Van Dorn and part of the Second Cavalry, who intended to establish a post in present Oklahoma. In a battle which occurred in the Wichita Mountains Ross was seriously wounded by the Comanche Mohee, who was killed. Van Dorn was also wounded.

The Indian scouts brought Ross back in a litter lashed between two mules; when that became too painful they carried him on their shoulders. Later Ross recalled:

> For their services Major Van Dorn gave the Indians of my command the captured spoils. I received for my pay a dangerous gunshot wound, together with a petition signed on the battlefield by every United States officer present requesting my appointment by the Government in the Army for distinguished gallantry, and after a time came a complimentary order from Gen. Winfield Scott.

Ross rescued a white girl, whom he named for Lizzie Tinsley, his fiancee; he raised Lizzie Ross to maturity after efforts to locate her family failed.

Because of his demonstrated ability, in September, 1860, Governor Houston ordered Ross to raise a company for frontier service. In the campaign which followed, Cynthia Ann Parker, who had been taken captive by Indians 24 years earlier, was recovered from the Comanche.

At Dallas, in September, 1861, he joined the 6th Texas Cavalry as a private. As a regimental major, under General Ben McCulloch, he fought the Creek Indians. At the battle of Elk Horn, in Arkansas, Ross' commander was his old friend, General Earl Van Dorn. In early 1862, at Corinth, Mississippi, Ross became colonel of the regiment, and after a year he was commanding a brigade composed of the 6th Texas and 1st Mississippi. After his promotion to general, Ross' Brigade was made up of the 3rd, 6th, 9th, and 27th Texas regiments and units from Tennessee, Mississippi and Missouri. He served throughout the Civil War and took part in 135 engagements.

Ross was farming near Waco, in 1873, when he was elected sheriff of McLennan County in a local attempt to combat the lawlessness afflicting Texas. He was quite effective and was succeeded by his brother, and deputy, Peter Ross. After service as a delegate to the Constitutional Convention of 1876, Ross farmed. He was a state senator when the capitol burned in November, 1881.

Ross' opponents for the 1886 Democratic gubernatorial nomination included Comptroller W. J. Swain, Major J. T. Breckenridge, D. C. Giddings, and former lieutenant governor Marion Martin, the "Swamp Fox of Navarro." (A most damaging allegation was that Swain wanted to use Indiana—not Texas—limestone in the new capitol.) At the Galveston convention Ross easily won the nomination.

Lawrence Sullivan Ross served as the nineteenth governor from January 18, 1887 to January 20, 1891.

Francis Lubbock said, "He was patriotic, honest, and devoted to the public interest." The *Galveston News* noted:

> General Ross is a good-looking man. . . . His face tells the nature of the man, which is that he would stick to his friends to death. He stands straight as an arrow and is not far from six feet high. . .his general appearance did not denote perfect health. General Ross is no orator. He is not even an ordinarily good speaker. He has a camp meeting drawl and the intonations of his voice sound unpleasant.

Jim Hogg was nominated to be attorney general and former governor Francis Lubbock was chosen for comptroller.

The Republican gubernatorial candidate, Dr. A. M. Cochran, of Dallas, favored a prohibition election if the people so desired. E. R. Dohoney, of the Prohibition party, claimed Ross was "a saloon stump speaker" who hoped to be "governor of a Christian people," and demanded a vote on prohibition. (A prohibition amendment, submitted in August, 1887, was badly beaten.) Ross attracted 228,776 ballots to Cochran's 65,236 and Dohoney's 19,186. The *Galveston News* was satisfied by the new governor's inaugural speech but believed it would not suit "those who expected to hear something about the stars singing together, and stuff of that kind, for it was read without any attempt to be oratorical."

During the Ross administration improvements were made in the system of selling and leasing public lands. Some 3.5 million acres of school, university, and asylum land were sold. In 1890 the land commissioner noted that "never before in the history of the west has settlement and development been so rapid as in the last two years. The unprecedented number of new counties which have organized demonstrates this." Applications for the purchase of state land for homes numbered from 40 to 75 a day.

Important steps were taken against the railroads' conspiracy to set rates, although the Railroad Commission was not established until Jim Hogg's time. In Ross' first year 964 miles of track were laid, and by the close of that term more than 8,000 miles of rail were in service. Slight regulation was being attempted, and Governor Coke's commission idea was gaining favor, although Ross did not believe such a body would be effective. Regulation was a big issue in the 1890 election, when the constitution was amended to provide for the Railroad Commission.

Ross presided over the dedication of the new capitol, which was begun in John Ireland's time, and his second inauguration took place there on January 15, 1889.

Ross became president of Texas A. & M. in 1891; it was not certain then that the institution could survive, but parents, unconvinced about the college, wanted their sons to study under Ross. He was responsible for the early success of A. & M. The student newspaper, The *Battalion*, for many years carried his name on its masthead, as "soldier, statesman, and knightly gentleman." Ross died at his home near Bryan on January 3, 1898. Sul Ross State University is named for him. The *Galveston News* assessed his qualities in this fashion:

> He was not masterful in the arts of politics, but, better than this, he was a well-balanced man from whatever standpoint one might estimate him. In his public relations he exhibited sterling common sense, lofty patriotism, inflexible honesty, and, withal, a character so exalted that he commanded at all times not only the confidence, but the affection of the people.

General Ross took part in 135 Civil War engagements.

Governors Lubbock, Roberts, Ross and Hogg all employ some variation of the Napoleonic hand-inside-the-coat pose.

Governor Francis Lubbock, Senator John Reagan, Confederate Brigadier General and United States Minister to Turkey A. W. Terrell, and Governor James Stephen Hogg; no more than five years has passed since the photograph on the opposite page was made, but the Napoleonic stance is no longer used.

Jim Hogg Was Born in Texas

James Stephen Hogg, "the People's Governor," was born near Rusk, Cherokee County, on March 4, 1851. His mother died a few months after the death of his father, General Joseph Lewis Hogg, in 1862, at Corinth, Mississippi. Jim Hogg worked on the family farm, had a year of schooling in Alabama, and at seventeen was setting type in a newspaper office. After calling him "a warrior of peacetime" and "apostle of a new economic civilization," Hugh Fitzgerald wrote, "He was for the under dog when the under dog had a grievance."

At the age of eighteen Hogg was shot in the back by a man he had helped the Wood County sheriff to arrest. During his weeks of convalescence he decided to become a lawyer, but first he was a printer's devil on a Tyler newspaper and, at twenty, he started the *Longview News*. While publishing the *Quitman News* Hogg became a justice of the peace in the 1873 election that ended the rule of E. J. Davis. Admitted to the bar, Hogg failed in a race for the legislature; it was the only loss of his political career. At the close of his term as Wood County Attorney, in 1880, he began building a reputation as an aggressive district attorney. He was fearless and impartial. Of that time Mary Barksdale wrote:

> ...there were existent a number of powerful corporations enjoying almost complete immunity from the law, and becoming daily more brazenly defiant of all attempts to control them. The evils of the practices of these bodies became so tremendous as to menace the future safety and peace of the commonwealth. So outspoken were Hogg's opinions of these companies and their practices, and so fearless were his attacks upon them when given an opportunity by the limited choices of his limited office, that the opinion of the public stamped him as the best district attorney in the state of Texas.

Hogg was elected attorney general in 1886. As the state's chief legal officer he recovered some 1.5 million acres of land which had been acquired through fraud. He fought the abuses of the great corporations and advocated regulation of the railroads. Addressing the issue "Shall the people or the corporations rule Texas?", in 1890 the voters made Jim Hogg governor, and by a count of 129,391 to 71,673 they authorized a railroad commission.

Texans liked the way Jim Hogg looked and talked. He was a huge man—a great fat common man with a great fat common name—who said things such as, "I'll put a head on them roosters as big as a barn."

The opposition began seeking a candidate to defeat him, for as Arthur Smith put it,

> In Texas, in 1892, the railroads and the so-called big corporations were on the verge of obtaining complete control of the State government. The corporations were a minor factor in the situation. It was the railroads, and notably Collis P. Huntington's Southern Pacific, which threatened to transform Texas into a feudal appendage of their legal departments, exactly as Huntington had done in the case of California.

Many Texans were uneasy about the Railroad Commission, believing that too much power had been given that appointive body. Although Texas governors usually received a second term, Hogg was in danger of losing. E. M. House, of Houston,

James S. Hogg, the twentieth governor, served from January 20, 1891 to January 15, 1895.

a rich man who understood Texas politics better than anyone else, volunteered his aid. House taught that "Politics is largely a question of organization. You've got to have a good, clean feller to put before the voters. After that it's organization." With railroads, banks and most businessmen arrayed against his candidate, House turned to the farmers and rural newspapers; he sent volunteers into the counties to work for the election of Hogg delegates to the convention. The major newspapers fought Hogg, who was, according to the *Galveston News*, "the czar and the autocrat of Texas, this completest and most perfect specimen of the demagogue that the nineteenth century and all of the other centuries have produced."

George Clark, a respected Waco attorney, became the candidate of Hogg's enemies. A former Confederate from Alabama, Clark had been secretary of state and attorney general under Richard Coke. Clark said he would "Turn Texas Loose." He and Hogg made a joint appearance before 8,000 people at Cameron. Many had come by special train, and all were partisan. More than 20,000 Texans were present at Cleburne. They were so unruly that only a few people actually heard the candidates, but Hogg did something there that Texans talked about for years. A few minutes after Clark paused in his speech and poured a glass of water, the massive Jim Hogg picked up the pitcher and drank from it, to the delight of his followers. The bleachers collapsed under 2,000 people, injuring several seriously, but the speaking continued after the casualties were cleared away.

The spirited campaign resulted in many counties sending two delegations—one for Hogg and one for Clark—to the Democratic convention. The Houston car barns had been remodeled to seat 8,000 delegates. As the sessions began neither side was willing to compromise. Each faction behaved as if its nominee for temporary chairman had won. Clark partisans lifted Jonathan Lane to the platform beside the Hogg representative. Grady St. Clair wrote that

> Each faction was apparently content with one half of the stage. With that much settled each chairman entered into the work of organization, paying no attention to the other. Each chairman made his speech of welcome and committees were appointed and heard from. Each faction loudly proclaimed itself the pure democracy of Texas.

Lieutenant Governor Barry Miller recalled, "I can see it as plainly as if it had been yesterday—Finley on one corner of the platform and Lane on the other—each conducting his own convention—and probably fifty fist fights in progress at the same time."

In the end the Clark people met separately and anointed their favorite; later the Republicans endorsed Clark for the general election. The state press, with the exception of the Tyler paper and the *Houston Post*, was doing its best for Clark. Hogg received 190,480 votes to Clark's 133,395. Thomas L. Nugent, of the People's Party, polled a surprising 108,483.

Hogg was broke and in debt when he left office, but by making good investments—including involvement in the Spindletop boom—as he practiced law, he was a wealthy man when he died on March 3, 1906, at Houston. He married Sallie Stinson. Their children, Mike, Will, and Ima Hogg made substantial contributions to the state. Jim Hogg County was created in 1913.

Jim Hogg, as photographed by "McLeod of Happy Hollow" in Arkansas.

This replica of his birthplace is located in Jim Hogg State Park at Rusk.

Jim Hogg, William Jennings Bryan, and friends on a hunting trip in South Texas.

Culberson Spent 32 Years in Public Life

Charles A. Culberson was the son of David B. Culberson, for whom Culberson County was named; he represented a Texas congressional district for 24 years. (When Congressman S. W. T. Lanham complained about the $5,000 salary, David Culberson said, "Sam, it may be inadequate, but it is powerful regular.") Charles Culberson, born in Alabama on June 10, 1855, was brought to Texas in infancy. He graduated from V.M.I. and the University of Virginia and practiced law at Jefferson with his father. He married Sally Harrison, and they moved to Dallas in 1887.

Culberson's race for attorney general grew out of a visit by gubernatorial candidate Jim Hogg, who knew that Culberson favored establishment of a railroad commission. (The Democratic convention that nominated Culberson also chose George Pendleton—an able, but unhandsome, man—for lieutenant governor. Pendleton's acceptance speech was interrupted by a delegate who shouted, "It's a damn good thing we nominated you before we saw you.") Culberson was an active attorney general because the quantity and nature of new legislation—railroad regulation and anti-trust laws—generated much litigation. His main achievement was the successful defense of the statute which created the Railroad Commission.

Jim Hogg believed Culberson, his successor as governor, to be "of a disposition to do justice to the people." With the support of Colonel E. M. House, Culberson defeated Populist T. L. Nugent in 1894; his lieutenant governor was George Jester, of Corsicana. Governor Culberson opposed national prohibition, believing that liquor regulation should be reserved to the states. In 1895 he convened the legislature to prohibit prize-fighting after plans had been made for the Jim Corbett-Bob Fitzsimmons match to be held in Dallas before a crowd of 53,000. Calling the event "a public display of barbarism," Culberson had stated that it was illegal. When a court held that prize fighting did not violate the law, he summoned the legislature, and a bill was passed declaring participation in "a pugilistic encounter between man and man" to be an offense punishable by two to five years in prison. James J. Corbett wrote:

> . . .everything was breezing along nicely, Fitzsimmons training at Corpus Christi. . .I in San Antonio, when we had trouble from an unexpected quarter. . . .But after the promoter had spent a fortune on the big arena, and interest in the fight had been worked up to the highest pitch, the Governor, just as a grandstand play. . .declared we could not fight in Texas. We did not object at all to a man doing his duty as he saw it, but we wished that he had seen this duty a little sooner, and before we had wasted so much money in our preparations.

The match was moved to Carson City, Nevada, where Fitzsimmons defeated Corbett. Later Culberson used the Rangers to keep the Fitzsimmons-Pete Maher fight from being held in Texas. It finally took place across the Rio Grande from Langtry.

Culberson won reelection in 1896. Populist Jerome C. Kearby, of Dallas, attracted 238,692 votes to Culberson's 298,528. When the Spanish-American War began, the state was asked to furnish four infantry regiments and one of cavalry. Colonel W. H.

Charles A. Culberson, the twenty-first governor, served from January 15, 1895 to January 17, 1899.

Mabry, of the First Infantry—the only Texas regiment to leave the United States—died of fever in Cuba.

Culberson spoke at the unveiling of a Confederate monument in 1897; Mrs. Stonewall Jackson and Jefferson Davis' daughter were present. During his administration the San Jacinto battlefield, neglected throughout the preceding 62 years, was purchased by the state. A uniform system of textbooks was adopted. Their prices had been, according to Culberson's secretary, "enormously high, and there is no doubt that a great many children have been deprived of the benefits of our free schools for no other reason than that their parents were too poor to pay the high prices demanded for school books." The system allowed old textbooks to be traded in on new ones and reduced the cost by 40%.

Culberson was sent to the United States Senate in 1899. A member of the committee which informed him of his election was John Nance Garner, Franklin Roosevelt's vice president in 1932. After 24 years in the Senate, Culberson died at Washington on March 19, 1925.

When a friend advised Culberson to use the "senator" title since that was a higher office than governor, Culberson protested, "I rather doubt that a United States Senatorship is a higher position than that of the Governor of Texas." His office displayed photographs of his three heroes, Thomas Jefferson, Robert E. Lee, and his father. In 1898, Culberson urged his father to run for the Senate, but the congressman said, "No, Charley, you are the man the people want, not me."

Culberson, as Democratic minority leader in 1907, was described as:

> He stands straight up and down and carries his head with mathematical deference to base and equilibrium. It is not impossible that to some, at first glance, he suggests a rather slim, rather wiry, not in the least overgrown New England clergyman from the rural districts. . . .

He was defeated by Ku Klux Klan candidate Earle Mayfield, in 1922. He was too ill to campaign actively for his fifth term. This was how he then appeared: "The venerable Senator Culberson. . .who could remember the antebellum period of his state, was so crippled by palsy as to be a pathetic figure, invariably in his seat, attentive to what went on but powerless to assume the leadership for which his experience fitted him."

The *New York World*, in 1922, noted

> For 63 years, the Culbersons, father and son, have served the State of Texas. . . . At last, on an issue of religious bigotry, a Culberson has been beaten in Texas. . . . The victor is the candidate of the Ku-Klux-Klan. . . .ostensibly it is a victory for the "native" over the "foreign" element. In fact, it is the temporary success of a mood of bigotry over the older and finer, over the truly native traditions of Texas. For it is the Culbersons who really represent what is native to Texas. . .and it is the Klan, with its masks and its imperial titles and its appeal to hatred, which is imported, the alien and un-American influence. Charles A. Culberson. . .was the darling of Texas politics. More than Bailey and longer than Houston he was the beloved leader of the Lone Star State. For thirteen years after his health failed Texas kept him in the Senate as a matter of pride. . . .

The efforts of Governor Culberson against prize fights were thwarted by Judge Roy Bean's help in holding the Bob Fitzsimmons-Pete Maher fight across the Rio Grande from Langtry.

Sayers Was Governor of the Catastrophes

Joseph Draper Sayers was born in Grenada, Mississippi, on September 23, 1841. His family moved to Bastrop when he was ten years old. He graduated from Bastrop Military Institute in 1860—Sam Houston, Jr. was a classmate and Governor Houston handed out the diplomas—and wanted to enter West Point, but secession was too near. He admired Sam Houston and agreed with his position on secession, but when the war began he joined a cavalry regiment as a private. By 1864 he was a major on General Thomas Green's staff. Because he did not allow serious wounds to keep him from duty, Francis Lubbock once introduced him to a Democratic convention as the only man he ever saw on a battlefield using two crutches.

Sayers taught school while reading law and began practice with George W. "Wash" Jones in 1866. An active Mason, he rose to be Grand Master of Texas. He married Ada Walton in 1868; she died in 1871, and he married her sister, Orline Walton. Sayers was elected to the state Senate in 1872. (This was the legislature that began liberating Texas from the radicals.) He became lieutenant governor in 1879. During his single term he and Governor Roberts had pronounced differences, especially on disposition of the public domain. Sayers was elected to the Congress in 1885 and served until January 17, 1899, when he was inaugurated as governor.

Sayers' main opponent for the Democratic nomination was M. M. Crane; as attorney general he appeared to have first refusal on the governorship, since recent attorneys general had succeeded to that office. But E. M. House, who had handled campaigns for Jim Hogg and Charles Culberson, decided that pattern should be broken and he chose Sayers for that purpose. By the time the convention opened, Sayers had shown formidable strength, and Crane had withdrawn. In the general election Sayers overwhelmed the Populist Barnett Gibbs and Prohibitionist Randolph Clark, of Waco, who drew 1,876 votes. Sayers told a *Dallas News* reporter:

> I have forty-seven years in this state. I came here a barefooted boy, before a mile of railroad or telegraph line was constructed and I could have bought, if I had had the money, every foot of ground upon which Dallas now stands at twenty-five cents per acre.

The Huntsville penitentiary burned and a devastating flood of the Brazos River took place in 1899. Heavy rains caused the Brazos to inundate about 12,000 square miles. The damage was estimated at $9 million, 284 people were killed, and thousands were without homes. Governor Sayers handled the collection and disbursement of relief funds, as he did after the Galveston flood.

Early in the morning of September 8, 1900, a storm which had crossed the Gulf of Mexico struck Galveston. By four o'clock from one to five feet of water covered the entire city, and Galveston Island was cut off from the outside world. Later, the wind, reaching about 120 miles an hour, swept the island with a six-foot tidal wave. The dead numbered between 5,000 and 8,000; no more accurate count was possible. Most of the animals were killed, and few buildings escaped damage. A large part of Galveston was

Joseph Sayers, the twenty-second governor, served from January 17, 1899 to January 20, 1903.

simply obliterated, as wrecked boats and buildings washed back and forth across the island and knocked down everything in their path.

Governor Sayers asked the Army for 10,000 tents and 50,000 rations. The food was sent, but fewer than 1,000 tents were immediately available. Clara Barton sent a telegram from Washington asking "Do you need the Red Cross in Texas? We are ready." Miss Barton collapsed while helping in Galveston; it was the last time she worked in the field. By September 14, Sayers had received almost $1 million in contributions. Messages of condolence came to him from people—including the German kaiser—all over the world. The impossibility of digging graves in cemeteries covered with six inches of silt, and the huge number of dead, made it necessary that the bodies be burned. On September 19, Sayers estimated the deaths in Galveston and elsewhere on the coast to be at least 12,000. About $40,000 a day was being spent for relief, and 4,000 men were clearing away wreckage and searching the debris for bodies. Workers were paid $1.50 a day; no able-bodied man was exempted from the task except those in the process of reopening their stores.

Efforts to rebuild Galveston caught the attention of the nation. Capitalizing on this interest Sayers invited a delegation of New York businessmen to visit Texas and consider investment possibilities. In May, 1901—four months before his assassination—President William McKinley and his wife were entertained in Austin by the governor. McKinley went on to Houston, where he spoke to the Daughters of the Republic of Texas and met Mrs. Mary Jones, the widow of Texas' last President. He conferred with the President of Mexico at El Paso.

After leaving office Sayers practiced law in San Antonio and Austin. He was a University of Texas regent during the Ferguson troubles and was chairman of the Industrial Accident Board. He died May 15, 1929, in Austin, and is buried in Bastrop.

Governor Sayers had served many years in the United States House of Representatives.

Lanham Prosecuted Satanta and Big Tree

The last Confederate to serve as governor of Texas was Samuel Willis Tucker Lanham. Born at Spartanburg, South Carolina, on July 4, 1846, Lanham was in the Army throughout the Civil War. He joined Kershaw's Brigade at fifteen, was wounded at Spottsylvania, and surrendered at Greensboro, North Carolina. In 1866 he married Sarah Meng, and they came by wagon train to Red River County, where their first child was born and died. They settled in Weatherford in 1868. The Lanhams taught school in one room of their log cabin. Tuition for a term of twenty weeks was from $2 to $4 per month, depending upon the level of the work. His education was meager, and each night Mrs. Lanham would teach him the things he would need to know for the next day. At the same time Lanham was studying law. He was admitted to the bar in 1869, and E. J. Davis made him attorney for the "Jumbo" district, which included most of West Texas.

On the day following his 25th birthday, Lanham prosecuted Satanta and Big Tree for murder. In May, 1871, a Kiowa war party had attacked Henry Warren's wagon train between Jacksboro and Fort Griffin and killed seven teamsters. Satanta—who had bragged about his part in the raid—Big Tree, and Satank were arrested at Fort Sill by Colonel Ranald Mackenzie. On the way to Jacksboro for trial, Satank attacked his guard and was killed. Lanham, whose closing argument was published in school books for use in declamation contests, told the jury:

> Satanta, the veteran chief of the Kiowas, the orator, the diplomat, the counselor of his tribe, the pulse of his race, we recognize in him the arch-fiend of treachery and blood, the promoter of strife. . . . In Big Tree we perceive the tiger-demon—the mighty warrior athlete, with the speed of a deer and eye of the eagle—who has tasted blood and loves it, who is swift at every species of ferocity and pities not at any sight of agony or death. He can scalp, burn, torture, mangle and deface his victims with all the superlatives of cruelty, and have no feelings of sympathy or remorse. . . .
> We have proven beyond a doubt that these prisoners were present when the seven teamsters were murdered, scalped, mutilated and burned, and that they boasted of what they had done. By their own words let them be condemned.
> Their conviction and punishment cannot repair the loss nor avenge the death of the good men they have slain, but it is due to law, justice and humanity that they should receive the highest punishment.

Defense lawyers Thomas Ball and Joe Woolfolk did their best, but there was no question of the braves' guilt. Their death sentences were commuted, and Satanta committed suicide in the penitentiary at Huntsville. After a few years in prison, Big Tree became a Baptist deacon and lived near Anadarko, Oklahoma.

In 1882 Lanham was elected congressman of the 98-county Eleventh District, which extended from Weatherford to El Paso; he liked to say that the 120,000-square-mile constituency was "bounded on the west by the Grace of God." Leaving Congress in 1892, Lanham practiced law in Weatherford. He tried for the 1894 Democratic gubernatorial nomination, but the convention chose Charles Culberson. Lanham

Samuel W. T. Lanham, the twenty-third governor, served from January 20, 1903 to
January 15, 1907.

returned to Congress in 1896, and after three terms he was nominated for governor to succeed former congressman Joseph Sayers. He was elected governor over the Republican George W. Burkett, of Anderson, and Socialist, Prohibitionist, and Populist candidates.

In his last session in Congress, Lanham voted against making assassination of the President a federal offense. He believed that all men were equal under the law and that a murder prosecution was always adequate without regard to the victim's identity. Because of the defeat of this bill—which resulted from the shooting of William McKinley—there was no federal statute when John Kennedy was killed in Dallas in 1963.

Lanham was inaugurated on January 20, 1903, with Lieutenant Governor George Neal. Pat Neff was elected speaker of the House. During Lanham's years the College of Industrial Arts, at Denton, and Southwest Texas Normal School, at San Marcos, opened. Other state institutions of higher education then in existence were the University of Texas, established in 1883; Texas A & M, 1876; Prairie View State Normal, 1879; Sam Houston Normal Institute, at Huntsville, in 1879, and North Texas State Normal, which was first funded by the state in 1901.

Lanham had a relatively quiet, peaceful four years. An important anti-trust act was passed, and the Terrell Election Law of 1903 changed the method of choosing officials. Until then conventions chose nominees under a loose system which lent itself to boss rule and fraud. The new law set voting qualifications, established the form to be used for ballots, required voting booths, provided a uniform method of holding primary elections, and designated the second Saturday in July for primaries and conventions. The 1905 election law was more detailed than its predecessor; it made the primary the nominating device for the Democratic party and restricted the convention to smaller parties.

In 1904 Governor Lanham was easily reelected over Republican James G. Lowden. He filed the sworn statement of expenditures required by the Terrell law showing his actual expenses had been $20. He wrote:

> I was very happy for years and years seeing the people in my district as their congressional representative. Then I became governor. Office-seekers, pardon-seekers, and concession-seekers overwhelmed me. They broke my health and when a man finds his health gone, his spirit is broken.

Mrs. Lanham died on July 2, 1908, and Lanham died July 29. His son, Fritz Garland Lanham, represented the Fort Worth-Weatherford district in Congress for 27 years.

Lanham was the last Confederate soldier to serve as governor of Texas.

Joe Bailey Proclaimed "The Campbells Are Coming"

The first two natives to become governor were born on adjoining farms near Rusk, Cherokee County: Jim Hogg on March 24, 1851, and Thomas Mitchell Campbell on April 22, 1856. They were boyhood friends. When Campbell announced his candidacy for governor six weeks after Hogg's death, his program included an assault upon corporate privilege that would have gladdened his old neighbor.

Campbell attended Rusk Masonic Institute and managed a year in Trinity University, at Tehuacana, before having to withdraw because of finances. While working in the district clerk's office at Longview, he read law at night. He began his practice a few months before his marriage to Fannie Bruner, in 1878. During Jim Hogg's administration Campbell was appointed master in chancery and then receiver of the International and Great Northern Railroad. After the receivership was closed, in 1892, he became general manager of the railroad and moved to Palestine. Campbell returned to private practice in 1897. Politically he earned a reputation as a progressive. At the 1902 Democratic State Convention, Campbell insisted upon a plank forbidding "the employment of children under twelve years of age in factories using machines" instead of the weak suggestion of a law "for the protection of children of tender age from overwork" which had been offered.

Until 1906 candidates had been selected by convention, but the new Terrell Election Law limited the Democrats and other parties receiving more than 100,000 votes to nominations by primary. Campbell went into the 1906 campaign with the blessing of the dying Jim Hogg; he had flayed recent administrations for favoring railroads and the great corporate interests. Campbell's opponents included former attorney general Charles Bell, of Fort Worth, Judge M. M. Brooks, of Dallas, and Railroad Commissioner O. B. Colquitt. The result in Texas' first statewide primary was: Campbell, 90,345, Brooks 70,064, Colquitt 68,529, and Bell, 65,168. Since there was no majority and no runoff was provided by law, the Democratic nomination had to be made by the convention. There delegates were thrown into a frenzy by the speech of Joe Bailey, who had supported Brooks. Bailey, an orator of the stature of Edward Everett and William Jennings Bryan, used all of the techniques at his command as he recounted the seige of Lucknow. No one knew what he intended to do, but in such a close contest his endorsement would insure the nomination. When Bailey repeated the admonition given the Lucknow defenders, "Hold out, hold out just a little longer; the Campbells are coming," the partisans of Tom Campbell stampeded the convention.

Campbell was easily reelected in 1908, when the voters also approved submission—by 146,223 to 141,306—of a prohibition amendment to the constitution. During his administration, long-needed legislation regulating business and industry was passed, special efforts were made to enforce the anti-trust laws, and the practice of leasing convicts was abolished.

Campbell's second legislature was much more conservative than the first. When legislators failed to implement their party platform, he said:

116

Thomas Campbell, the twenty-fourth governor, served from January 15, 1907 to January 19, 1911.

Trainload jaunts over the State, frequent adjournments, filibustering, and the interference of a trained and organized lobby, sent here by selfish interests which combine in an effort to defeat all legislation in behalf of the masses of the people, have so far contributed to the failure of the Legislature to meet the full expectations of the people.

Campbell supported Woodrow Wilson for the presidency. In 1916 he ran for the Senate, but the governorship was the only office he ever held. Ralph Steen believed "He was not so good a governor as he thought he was, but he was a better governor than his enemies said he was." He died of leukemia on April 1, 1923, at Galveston and was buried in Palestine.

Tom Campbell, the second native Texan to serve as governor, was a boyhood friend of Jim Hogg, the first governor born in the state.

O. B. Colquitt Fought a Border War

Born December 16, 1861, in Mitchell County, Georgia, Oscar Branch Colquitt was the son of an impoverished Confederate soldier. His mother, a graduate of Wesleyan Female College, died in 1879, a year after the family came to Morris County, Texas. Colquitt started school at Daingerfield; his total education was only a few months, but while running a tenant farm he spent most of his spare time reading. Becoming active in county politics at the age of eighteen, he soon left the farm and "Got a job as a hod carrier, then as a porter at the Daingerfield depot, and did every other work I could find; then worked in a furniture factory, turning out bedposts." He became a *Morris County Banner* printer's devil at $12.50 a month, leaving his $1.25-a-day job at the factory because, "I am ambitious to be an editor or a lawyer." With his savings—$175—he started the *Pittsburg Gazette* in 1884. After selling the paper to his brother, he bought the *Terrell Star*. In 1890, after merging the *Times* with the *Star*, Colquitt supported Jim Hogg.

Colquitt was elected to the state Senate in 1894. (A losing candidate was William H. Murray, who became governor of Oklahoma.) Supporting a lower school tax rate, Colquitt wrote "School teachers of the state, as a rule, are tax eaters, not tax payers." That statement haunted him in each of his political campaigns. Because of his work on the tax laws Governor Culberson appointed him state revenue agent, and Governor Sayers made him a member of the tax commission. Colquitt was chairman of the group which located Texas Woman's University at Denton. (A major argument for choosing that city was a possible merger with North Texas Normal School.)

Colquitt, who had studied law over the years, began practice at Terrell in 1899. He succeeded the 83-year-old John Reagan on the Railroad Commission in 1903 and built an admirable reputation in the next eight years. In 1906, he ran for governor against Thomas Campbell, of Palestine, Judge M. M. Brooks, of the Dallas Court of Civil Appeals, and Attorney General Charles Bell, of Fort Worth. His opposition to statewide prohibition and the earlier statement about teachers were factors in his loss.

Colquitt sought, in 1910, to succeed Campbell. His competition included Cleburne attorney William Poindexter, Cone Johnson, of Tyler, and Attorney General Robert V. Davidson. Prohibition was the big issue. Colquitt favored local option but opposed statewide prohibition; Davidson proposed an election on the question, and the other two advocated statewide prohibition. The next most important issue—in this contest of irrelevancies—was Baileyism: the candidate's position on the integrity of Senator Joseph Weldon Bailey. Colquitt promised prison reform, including the abolition of whippings, which gave him an opportunity to demonstrate the bat, a brutal whip, formerly used at Huntsville, made of three-inch cowhide strips nailed to a large wooden handle. Colquitt, weighing 180 pounds, could barely wield the five-foot whip as he flogged an imaginary prisoner tied spread-eagled on the floor. George Huckaby, after researching his fine dissertation thirty years later, wrote that everyone he interviewed mentioned Colquitt's showing the bat. Despite Campbell's efforts against

Oscar B. Colquitt, the twenty-fifth governor, served from January 19, 1911 to January 19, 1915.

him, Colquitt prevailed, with 146,871 votes to Poindexter's 80,060, Johnson's 76,268, and Davidson's 53,366. By 154,609 to 125,809, voters approved submission of a constitutional prohibition amendment. (That amendment, in 1911, was voted down, 237,393 to 231,096.) In the general election Colquitt received 174,596 votes to Republican J. O. Terrell's 26,191, Socialist Redding Andrews' 11,538, and Prohibitionist Andrew Jackson Houston's 6,052 votes.

The most difficult of Colquitt's problems concerned the Mexican border. In 1910 revolution had broken out against Porfirio Diaz, who had been dictator since 1876, and the disorder spilled across the Rio Grande as bands of armed Mexicans invaded Texas to kill, steal and destroy. Colquitt was soon at odds with Washington over the lack of protection. In September, 1911, President Taft promised reimbursement for the state's expense in defense of lives and property along the border. Colquitt increased the Ranger force from 15 to 50 and ordered Mexican revolutionaries to leave within 48 hours. Taft sent troops, who argued with the Rangers over jurisdiction.

In Colquitt's first term there was a controversy over the textbook board's rejection of a history book containing Abraham Lincoln's photograph. Colquitt stated, "I want the truth of history taught. . . . I had rather resign the Governor's office of Texas than to have my children studying a textbook in the public schools of Texas with Abe Lincoln's picture left out of it, and I am the son of a Confederate soldier."

Although Texas governors usually have little difficulty in reelection, his efforts against the prohibition amendment made Colquitt's future uncertain. Supreme Court Justice William Ramsay, with prohibitionist backing—they called the governor Oscar Budweiser Colquitt—announced against him. Ramsay, a Trinity University classmate of Governor Campbell, had been Attorney General M. M. Crane's law partner. Once again Colquitt demonstrated the bat, claiming to have banned its use in the penitentiary. He complained of county and city prisoners wearing iron balls chained to their ankles and working while their guards "snoozed in the shade of a building." Colquitt, the first to use the automobile extensively in a Texas campaign, spent 85 days on the stump.

Speaking to a huge picnic crowd at Hamilton, Ramsay drew prolonged applause and moved the band to play "Dixie" by eulogizing Confederate veterans. He said that Governor Campbell had stopped the use of the bat at the penitentiary a year before Colquitt took office. He pointed out his resignation from the Supreme Court to run for governor, while Colquitt still drew his $4,000-a-year salary. Most newspapers supported Ramsay, but Colquitt won the Democratic nomination, 215,808 to 179,857, and in the general election he overwhelmed, 234,352 to 25,253, the Socialist Redding Andrews, who ran well ahead of the Republican nominee and Prohibitionist Andrew Jackson Houston.

The border troubles worsened. Francisco Madero, who had overthrown Diaz, had been killed by General Huerta, who now held the government against General Carranza and others. The complaints of South Texans brought Colquitt into conflict with the Wilson administration.

As World War I began, Colquitt was anti-Wilson, anti-British, and pro-German, which did him little good when he tried to unseat three-term incumbent Charles A. Culberson in the state's first popular election for senator. Because of his bad health, Culberson's campaign was carried on by others. Although Colquitt led in the first primary, Culberson won the runoff. Colquitt supported Herbert Hoover in 1928. He was working for the Reconstruction Finance Corporation when he died on March 8, 1940. His wife, Alice Murrell Colquitt, died nine years later.

TURKEY TROT CUERO, TEX
GOV. COLQUITT AND STAFF

Governor Colquitt and his staff got all dressed up to review the participants in Cuero's Turkey Trot. (Ruby Begonia, V, is the most recent local champion in this Great Gobbler Gallop.)

James Ferguson Was Removed From Office

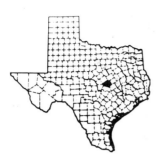

Born August 31, 1871, on a Bell County farm, James E. Ferguson, Jr., had only a rudimentary education. His father died when he was four, and he spent most of his childhood in the fields. Leaving home at sixteen, he traveled the western states, working at whatever he could find. He spent seven years on a bridge-building crew. Back in Bell County, he farmed, studied law, and began practicing at Belton, in 1897. His partnership with John D. Robinson flourished, and on the last day of '1899 he married Miriam Amanda Wallace.

Ferguson sold the Farmers State Bank, of Belton, which he had founded and served as president, and started the Temple State Bank. His experience in politics had been limited to assisting O. B. Colquitt and other candidates until, in 1913, he wrote a letter to a newspaper urging the election of a businessman governor and suggesting the candidacy of Tom Henderson, of Cameron. Many Texans—including Henderson—responded, and most stated that Ferguson should be the governor.

Because the prohibition issue had been given excessive attention, at the expense of significant problems, Ferguson promised to veto all bills presented to him on that subject. He hoped to improve rural schools, and he promised to limit farm rentals to a fourth of the cotton produced and a third of grain crops; the landlord would be entitled to half the crop if he furnished tools, implements, feed and teams. His opponent, former congressman Thomas Ball, of Houston, was a prohibitionist, which caused Ferguson to ask why Ball belonged to the Houston Club. When Ball stated that his interest in the organization was literary, Ferguson showed that in the past year the Houston club had spent only $112 for books and magazines but had bought $361.48 worth of cards and poker chips and purchased liquor costing $10,483.15.

Both Ferguson and Ball claimed to be in the Jim Hogg tradition. Ferguson was beginning to be called "Farmer Jim." In the Democratic primary, Ferguson got 237,062 votes to Ball's 191,558, and voters turned down the submission of a prohibition amendment. In the general election Ferguson polled 176,599 of the 214,781 ballots cast, and W. P. Hobby became lieutenant governor.

In his first administration Ferguson got along well with the legislature. Most of his program, including the limit on farm rentals, became law. Free textbooks were authorized when approved by school districts. The border had been violated regularly by Mexican raiders; after Pancho Villa's attack on Columbus, New Mexico, John J. Pershing led troops into Mexico. On May 9, 1916, Texas, New Mexico, and Arizona National Guard units were activated and sent to the Rio Grande. Ferguson praised President Wilson for calling up the guard. He believed the United States should invade Mexico and institute "that stability of government which they are now unable and helpless to establish. . . ."

At Ferguson's direction, the platform adopted by the 1916 Democratic State Convention opposed prohibition and woman's suffrage. Ferguson—whose wife would be the first woman elected to govern an American state—at the national convention delivered a minority report against suffrage, while women in the galleries hissed. His

James E. Ferguson became the twenty-sixth governor on January 19, 1915 and was removed by impeachment on August 25, 1917.

opponent in the primary, Charles Morris, ran a hard race, but Ferguson had done a good job, and by tradition Texas governors were entitled to two terms. Ferguson campaigned only briefly, while Morris punched the empty air. Later a few of the Morris allegations would be found to be true and would furnish some of the grounds upon which the governor was impeached. Ferguson attracted 237,869 out of 414,000 votes, but this time the Democrats voted for submission of a prohibition amendment.

At Ferguson's request, substantial appropriations were made for rural schools. The legislature established agricultural junior colleges at Stephenville (now Tarleton State University) and Arlington (the University of Texas at Arlington) and appropriated funds for a West Texas A. & M. (After some problems Lubbock was chosen as the site.) The state bought East Texas Normal, which is now East Texas State University, and created Stephen F. Austin Teachers College and Sul Ross State Normal College. The Highway Commission was established, making it possible for Texas to receive federal road funds. A commission was founded to administer the laws providing free school books. Although Ferguson supported Woodrow Wilson's preparedness program, at the outset he was against the draft.

Disagreement over interpretation of the appropriation for the University of Texas in 1915 had developed into a contest of wills between Ferguson and the regents and administration. The governor demanded that President R.E. Vinson fire some professors and otherwise tried to interfere with the university's internal management. Problems with the university caused Ferguson's impeachment, although he was convicted on other charges, too. After the House passed a bill of 21 articles of impeachment, on August 25, 1917, W. P. Hobby became acting governor. The three-week trial in the Senate resulted in Ferguson's conviction on ten of the articles, including: (1) paying a personal note with West Texas State Normal College funds, (2) depositing, at no interest, state money in banks partially owned by him, (3) depositing $250,000 of state money in an Austin bank to the credit of Temple State Bank, (4) receiving about $156,000 from sources he refused to identify, (5) trying to get professors discharged, without cause, and attempting to get rid of some regents. Judgment was entered on September 25, 1917, removing the governor and disqualifying him from ever holding office. (Ferguson, having resigned the preceding day, always contended that the prohibition was ineffective; since he held no office he was not subject to the Senate's jurisdiction when the judgment was made.)

Ferguson remained a factor in state politics, and his wife was twice elected governor.

Jim Ferguson makes his inaugural address. Lieutenant Governor Hobby is seated to his left.

Will Hobby Was a Newspaperman

William Pettus Hobby was born March 26, 1878, at Moscow, Livingston County. His Confederate veteran father, District Judge Edwin Hobby, moved the family to Houston when he was fourteen; two years later Hobby quit school and went to work in the circulation department of the *Houston Post*. He was much impressed by William Sydney Porter—O. Henry—and other reporters. Moving from job to job, Hobby finally became the *Post*'s managing editor. In 1907 he took over the *Beaumont Enterprise,* which flourished under his management; within a few years Hobby bought it. He was quite active in civic affairs, and through his efforts Beaumont became a deep-water port.

In 1914 it appeared that prohibitionists would capture the state's top two offices. Hobby, believing with Jim Ferguson that the prohibition controversy distracted from more important issues, announced for lieutenant governor. He was elected over prohibitionist candidate B. B. Sturgeon, of Paris, and was unopposed for a second term. Hobby was the first Jefferson County citizen to hold a state office.

Governor Ferguson had many enemies, particularly among prohibitionists. When the United States entered World War I the prohibition controversy became more intense. In addition, Ferguson was under heavy attack by friends of the University of Texas. Upon Ferguson's impeachment, on August 24, 1917, Hobby became acting governor; after his conviction and removal, on September 25, Hobby served the balance of Ferguson's term.

Although Hobby had opposed statewide prohibition, he supported legislation forbidding liquor sales within ten miles of military installations. Army camps were so numerous that the legislation affected most of the state. In aid of the war effort, the legislature ratified the 18th amendment, sanctioning national prohibition, and forbade the manufacture and sale of intoxicants.

Hobby helped put the new Highway Department on a sound footing, which facilitated construction of badly-needed roads. He signed the bill giving women the right to vote, but his main concern was the war. Enlistments in the armed forces had to be encouraged, and troops were needed to take the place of the Texas National Guard, which was on active duty. In addition, Hobby had a multitude of obligations pertaining to military installations; one-seventh of all American servicemen were stationed in Texas. Nearly a million Texans registered for the draft; 198,000 served, and about 5,000 died in the armed forces.

Hobby sought a term of his own in 1918. Ignoring the judgment barring him from office, Jim Ferguson ran. Naturally the deposed governor resented his successor. Ferguson ridiculed his opponent's big ears and lack of height. Hobby answered, "I will admit that the Supreme Being failed to favor me with physical attributes pleasing to Governor Ferguson, but at least He gave me the intelligence to know the difference between my own money and that which belongs to the state." When Ferguson, objecting to the construction of tennis courts at the Mansion, suggested a cow lot instead, Hobby responded, "It's too bad that the ex-Governor didn't think of the milch

William P. Hobby, the twenty-seventh governor, succeeded Ferguson on August 25, 1917 and served until January 18, 1921.

cow pen while he was in office. They say in those days he confined his milking activities to the public treasury." Hobby's vote doubled Ferguson's, and he lost only 20 of the 254 counties.

Hobby was an influenza victim, but he made a prompt recovery. The state's high concentration of servicemen created serious problems during the epidemic; nearly 80% were sick, and some 9,000 died. Civilian losses were even higher. (The worldwide influenza death toll reached 21 million; the 350,000 who died in the United States were ten times more numerous than the Americans killed in the war.)

Texas women voted for the first time in the 1918 Democratic primary, and Annie Webb Blanton, chosen as Superintendent of Public Instruction, was the state's first woman official. In 1919, with Hobby's support, Texas became the first Southern state to ratify the women's suffrage amendment.

After leaving office Hobby returned to Beaumont. With purchase of the *Journal*, the *Enterprise*'s competitor, he had morning and evening coverage. In 1922 Hobby moved back to Houston; Ross Sterling, the owner of the *Houston Dispatch*, had bought the *Houston Post* and wanted Hobby to run them. While retaining ownership of the Beaumont papers, Hobby became president of the *Post-Dispatch*, which acquired radio station KPRC in 1925.

Hobby had married Willie Chapman Cooper in 1915. Her father, Samuel Bronson Cooper, had been a congressman for fourteen years. She died in 1929, and two years later Hobby married Oveta Culp, a former parliamentarian of the House of Representatives. In World War II, with the rank of colonel, she commanded the Women's Auxiliary Army Corps. She was the first Secretary of Health, Education and Welfare, in the Eisenhower administration. Sterling, while governor, lost most of his wealth and had to sell the *Post-Dispatch*. The new owner, J. E. Josey, let Hobby change the name to the *Houston Post*. The paper supported Sterling in his 1932 reelection campaign, but Mrs. Ferguson defeated him. The *Post* favored repeal of prohibition. Hobby bought the *Houston Post* in 1939 and fought Franklin Roosevelt's third term. Mrs. Hobby was elected president of the *Houston Post* Company, in 1955, and Hobby became chairman of the board. He died in Houston on June 7, 1964, nine years before his son became lieutenant governor.

Kittrell wrote that:

> William P. Hobby has borne himself so meekly in his great office as to have deserved the plaudits bestowed upon him by the great tribunal of the party—the State Convention.
>
> As I have said before, Texas has been most fortunate in the matter of Governors. All of them may not have been men intellectually pre-eminent, but none has ever been the tool of any ring, or been subservient to sinister influences, and every one, save one, took and laid down his trust with clean hands, a record of which any Texan should be proud.

Chief Justice Nelson Phillips administers the oath of office to Lieutenant Governor
Hobby as Governor Ferguson watches.

Pat Neff Was a Straight Arrow

Pat Morris Neff was born November 26, 1871, on a McLennan County farm: when later he made a campaign speech at nearby McGregor he pledged his best efforts to Texas, saying, "In truth, I can say to her what Agnes said to David Copperfield: 'I have loved you all my life.' " He was ten years old when his father died, leaving nine children. Neff graduated from McGregor High School and Baylor University. His law degree was conferred in 1897, and he began practice in Waco.

Neff was elected to the legislature in 1900. Old Baylor friend Tom Connally—later a United States Senator—and John Nance Garner—later Vice President of the United States—were representatives. That legislature sent Joseph Weldon Bailey to the Senate to replace the incumbent, Horace Chilton. In 1903 Neff, nominated by Connally, became speaker of the House.

Neff was elected McLennan County Attorney and served six years. An outstanding prosecutor, he lost only sixteen of 422 criminal cases. For four years the fines paid in Neff's cases exceeded the total collected in the other 253 counties. Neff believed the main deterent to crime was not the severity, but the certainty, of punishment. He was the first county attorney to send a bootlegger to the penitentiary.

After eight years in private practice, he announced for governor in 1920. He wrote:

> No one solicited me to run for governor. I did not ask permission of anyone to get into the race. Just as a freeborn American, and as a native son of Texas, without a conference with or advice from anyone, I announced my candidacy.

Attorney General Ben Looney, Speaker of the House R. E. Thomason, of El Paso, and former senator Joseph Weldon Bailey, of Gainesville, were his opponents. Bailey denounced President Wilson, prohibition and "women voting." Texas "had gone to seed", but he thought he could effect a cure.

Neff canvassed places traditionally ignored by candidates.

> The entire campaign was one big bright day. I enjoyed it all—the dew of the morning, the fierce heat of high noon, the resplendent beauties of the victorious eventide. . . . To speak to an audience composed of the enthusiastic supporters of another was my greatest delight. Calling sinners to repentance. . .was my political creed.

Neff spoke 850 times and in 37 counties which had never been visited by a gubernatorial candidate; one of these was Webb, whose capital, Laredo, was more than a century and a half old. Not since Sam Houston—65 years earlier—had anyone come to Leon County seeking the governorship. Neff was well received; his three to seven speeches a day in 152 counties and travel by airplane, automobile and mule made him the "wild man from Waco." Kittrell recalled that, "He took his Ford and was his own chauffeur, and went directly to the people, frankly and unreservedly declaring himself on every public question."

Since Bailey was the most interesting target, Neff concentrated on him. Noting

Pat Neff, the twenty-eighth governor, served from January 18, 1921 to January 20, 1925.

that Bailey did not approve of any living politician except himself, Neff concluded, "He praises the dead alone." Neff claimed history had produced three supreme egotists: "one was Napoleon and Senator Bailey the other two." Thomason said Neff had "never cocked a gun, fished on Sunday, nor used tobacco."

Bailey led the field by fewer than 2,000 votes in the first primary, but Neff won the runoff. Prior to inauguration he refused speaking engagements; he was tired of hearing himself. Pat Neff was the fifth native Texan, and the fifth college graduate, to become governor.

Neff, who had put so many criminals there, was worried about penitentiary conditions. The principal punishment was suspending convicts by chains attached to their wrists, their toes barely touching the floor, for as long as eight hours. Dogs were set on prisoners, who were otherwise mistreated and ill-fed. Prison commissioners paid exhorbitant amounts for horses and mules; the prison farms' records were inaccurate; and there was other evidence of fraud. Neff took steps to correct these abuses and those discovered at the reformatory.

The 34-mile railroad between Rusk and Palestine, which was owned by the prison system, had lost money for years; it owed the permanent school fund more than $130,000. Neff recommended that it be sold. The legislature leased it to the Texas and New Orleans, producing only a small rental but ending the operating losses.

In 1922 a strike idled some 1,400 railroad employees. Neff went to Denison and investigated without being recognized. (Some strikers told him there was plenty of work, but "none of you scabs need apply for it.") He decided Rangers could handle the situation, but the Harding administration threatened Army intervention if he did not send troops. Neff, "unwilling for federal troops to march on Texas soil for the purpose of enforcing Texas laws," declared martial law. The National Guard remained in Denison for three months.

The legislature gave Neff only slight cooperation in his efforts to economize. He approved the appropriations for education, which were the largest in history, but he vetoed the bill establishing West Texas A & M College because it conflicted with the Democratic platform. He believed officials elected on a party platform were bound by it. Responding to the veto the Democrats included the college in the 1922 platform, and Neff signed the bill creating Texas Technological College. South Texas State Teachers College, now Texas A&I University, was founded at Kingsville. Neff was renominated without a runoff. In the September convention Neff denounced the Ku Klux Klan, which had developed alarming strength; even so, Neff declared "The world is getting better. . .never before was our entire civilization so shot through with the lofty ideals of Christianity."

Neff's attempt to bring about a constitutional convention failed. He pointed out the absence of labor, capital, strike, and boycott problems in 1876 and quoted Thomas Jefferson, "Every constitution expires at the end of twenty years, and if it is enforced longer, it is an act of force, and not of right."

Governor Neff devoted much thought to the need for a workable system of justice. He charged that the value of everything in Texas was inflated "except human life; it is our cheapest commodity." While Texas had 200 homicides for every million citizens in 1922, Germany had twelve and Canada had five. Neff said:

> More people last year were murdered in Texas, with a population of five million, than were murdered during the past twenty years in the British Empire, with a population of fifty million. . . . We have in this

Governor Neff and his lady and former governor Hobby and Mrs. Hobby pose with a delegation from Mexico at Neff's inauguration.

country too many killings and too few convictions. In Germany, ninety-five per cent of those who take human life are convicted, in Texas, two per cent. In England few cases remain untried beyond ninety days, and if the case is appealed, it is passed on ordinarily within a month. It takes almost two years to dispose of the average hotly-contested criminal case in Texas, and about half the cases have to have a second trial at which the defendant, having worn out his case, is found not guilty.

Neff saw in lax enforcement of the prohibition statutes a threat to all law.

Neff made significant contributions in other areas. He started the state park system and laid the foundation for the Texas Centennial. At the inauguration of Mrs. Ferguson, Neff said that what was a crown of thorns when he took office had become "a garland of sweet forget-me-nots." He intended to take his place among the common people "where the great heart of humanity beats," and he gave this blessing to his successor: "May the God who guides the migratory birds in their flight and who holds within the hollow of His hand the destinies of men, guide and guard you, and hold and keep Texas aright."

Pat Neff was chairman of the Railroad Commission when the East Texas field—the world's largest—came in, and he helped institute proration to conserve oil and gas reserves. Although he had been elected president of the University of Texas and had declined to serve, he accepted the Baylor presidency in 1932 after having been chairman of the Baylor trustees for a quarter century. Baylor grew during his tenure, as depression-era problems gave way to the huge enrollments of World War II veterans.

Pat Neff married Myrtle Mainer, whom he had met while they were Baylor students, at her home in Lovelady, Texas. Neff died in Waco on January 20, 1952, and is buried in Oakwood Cemetery, beneath a stone inscribed, "I have worked and wrought as best I could to make Texas a better place in which to live." Mrs. Neff died in 1953.

Pat Neff Hall is a reminder of the president who did so much for Baylor University.

Mrs. Ferguson Was the First Woman Elected Governor

Miriam Amanda Wallace was born June 13, 1875, into a wealthy Bell County family. Her initials—M.A.W.—provided a nickname that helped make her governor—"Me for Ma"—although she forbade its use in her presence. She attended Salado College and Baylor Female College. On the last day of 1899, she married James Edward Ferguson, governor of Texas from 1915 until 1917.

The removal of Jim Ferguson and the prohibition against his holding public office caused his wife to enter politics. She said, soon after the conviction: "It is a terrible thing to be tried and sold down the river by politicians who have their price! But never fear, Jim Ferguson will come back!" Ouida Ferguson, blaming the impeachment on women's suffrage, which her father had resisted, wrote:

> Without even so much as paying the poll tax which had always been required of men, the women of Texas were allowed to vote by authority of a bill rushed through the legislature and signed by Governor Hobby before the primaries. The women turned out en masse and cast their votes for Hobby.

In 1918 Ferguson ran against Governor Hobby, despite the Senate judgment that he was "disqualified to hold any office of honor, trust, or profit, under the State of Texas." Hobby won. Voters concerned about the war remembered Ferguson's arguments against the draft, and his opposition to prohibition was not forgotten; the legislature had recently ratified the prohibition amendment. After he was refused a place on the ballot in 1924, his wife announced for governor. Texas would have two governors for the price of one, she promised. S. S. McKay wrote of the campaign:

> Mrs. Ferguson usually opened the rally with a short statement that she would be the real governor if elected and that Jim would be merely her right hand man. She would then admit that she was not an experienced public speaker and would give way to her husband. The former governor would then belabor the enemy with vigor. One local chairman introduced him by saying simply, "All you owls hunt your holes! The Eagle is here."

The big issue that year was Ku Klux Klan influence in government. The Fergusons denounced the Klan without restraint, and District Judge Felix Robertson, of Dallas, the KKK candidate, tried to focus attention on his support of prohibition. Mrs. Ferguson asked for help in vindicating Jim Ferguson, saying "A vote for me is a vote of confidence for my husband, who cannot be a candidate because his enemies have succeeded in barring him from holding public office." She was photographed at her birthplace wearing a borrowed sunbonnet and doing farm chores, resulting in the adoption of "Put on Your Old Gray Bonnet" as her campaign song; at her inauguration it was performed by Brownwood's Old Gray Mare Band. Mrs. Ferguson trailed Robertson, 146,424 to 193,508, in the first primary. She received 413,751 votes to Robertson's 316,019 in the runoff. The Republicans nominated George Butte, a University of Texas law professor, in another phase of the old battle between Jim

Miriam Ferguson, the twenty-ninth governor, was also the thirty-second governor. She served from January 20, 1925 to January 17, 1927 and from January 17, 1933 to January 15, 1935.

Ferguson and the university. Sam Acheson wrote: "The Republican candidate for governor was defeated by a close vote, and the Klan, denied control of the state government, began to pass into history as a statewide political factor."

Mrs. Ferguson became the first woman elected governor of an American state; however, Nellie Tayloe Ross, of Wyoming, elected later, was inaugurated first. Ouida Ferguson wrote of their return:

> All of us piled into the old twin-six Packard, with Mamma at the wheel. It was, incidentally, the very same car in which we had departed from the Governor's Mansion in 1917. As Mama pulled up the hand brake under the old Porte-cochere at the Mansion, the new governor of Texas said, as if addressing the old chariot: "Well, we have returned! We departed in disgrace; we now return in glory!"

Mrs. Ferguson was infuriated upon finding her name obliterated from the entrance of the greenhouse she had built; she hired a concrete man to restore her name and the original date. (A few years afterward Mrs. Dan Moody, appalled when a friend suggested removal of Mrs. Ferguson's name from the greenhouse, remarked that such an act might provoke Mrs. Ferguson into running again just to get her name put back.)

Attorney General Dan Moody defeated Mrs. Ferguson in 1926. She lost to Ross Sterling, in 1930, but frustrated his reelection. Her last race was in 1940. John Gunther wrote, in his *Inside U.S.A.*:

> In one period of twenty months, the Fergusons issued more than two thousand pardons; which was one way to build up popularity. Ma got in partly because she and Pa had courage enough to fight the Ku-Klux-Klan, which is to their credit. Ma ran for governor four times more (and Pa once ran for the Senate but got beat), and made it once, in 1933. . . . That the Fergusons had a good deal to do with O'Daniel's first victory and with Stevenson's is usually accepted. In other words, from the time of Jim Hogg fifty years ago to the present, the most conspicuous public figures in the biggest state in the union were little more than a pair of self-seeking old buffoons.

Jim Ferguson died September 21, 1944; Mrs. Ferguson survived until June 25, 1961. The inscription on their tombstone in the State Cemetery reads, "Life's race well run, Life's work well done, Life's victory won, Now cometh rest."

Mrs. Ferguson was the first woman elected to govern an American state.

Dan Moody Was the Youngest Governor

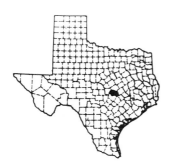

Daniel James Moody, Jr., born June 1, 1893, in Taylor, was the son of the town's first mayor. Moody held jobs during most of his school years. He was fifteen when his father died, but he graduated the next year and saved enough money while working as a telephone lineman to enter the University of Texas in 1910. After leaving the university, in 1914, he read law and practiced with Taylor attorney Harris Melasky.

Although he had a draft deferment because of his invalid mother's dependence, he enlisted as a private during World War I and was discharged after the war as a second lieutenant. While running for county attorney, in 1920, Moody also campaigned for gubernatorial candidate Pat Neff. Two years later Governor Neff appointed Moody district attorney.

The Ku Klux Klan, growing nationally at a terrifying rate, was particularly strong in Texas. Young District Attorney Moody was the first prosecutor in the country to engage the Klan and win. Soon after Moody took office, on Easter Sunday of 1923, R. W. Burleson, a salesman from Waco, and a young widow were riding with another couple when their car was stopped by masked men near Jonah. (Earlier the Georgetown Klan had warned Burleson not to see the lady again.) Several men dragged Burleson into another car, took him to a place where he was stripped, chained by the neck to a tree, whipped with a wide leather strap, and threatened with death. After he had been given about fifty blows and tar or creosote had been poured into his wounds, he was left on the City Hall grounds in Taylor chained to a tree. About 8:30 p.m. Burleson managed to get loose and seek help. Constable Louis Lowe, who had a machinist cut off the chain, said that Burleson was lacerated and bruised all over, that removal of the tar from his head and body was difficult and painful, and that Burleson was "as raw as a piece of beef from the small of his back to the knees; and in many places the skin had been split and the flesh was gaping open."

Moody successfully prosecuted Klansman Murray Jackson, who was given the maximum sentence of five years. (Mrs. Ferguson pardoned him two years later.) Olen Gossett and Dewey Ball pleaded guilty and received one year terms. The Baptist preacher, A. A. Davis, who had delivered the Klan's warning to Burleson, was convicted of perjury for lying to the grand jury and sentenced to two years.

Moody's handling of the cases attracted national attention. The *New York Herald* reported:

> Dan Moody made midnight whipping parties go out of style in his neighborhood. . . . About the time his term started, an epidemic of midnight floggings broke out all over Texas. The epidemic in the course of time touched Moody's district—but it did not spread there. . . . A traveling salesman was dragged from his car while touring the country with a woman, flogged, covered with the usual coating of tar and dumped out in the streets of Taylor, Williamson County. When Dan Moody went over to Taylor and said he was going to enforce the law there was not much interest at first, for folks had gotten used to such floggings and had never known of any prosecution. There were convictions, penitentiary

Dan Moody, the thirtieth governor, served from January 17, 1927 to January 20, 1931.

sentences, and affirmation of sentences on appeal. Members of the "whipping squad" are in prison; others are seeking to escape by a fight in the higher courts.

Admiring Texans made Moody the attorney general in 1924. The fact that he was only 31 bothered no one but his opponents. One of his important cases established that oil royalties from state university land were to be deposited in the permanent—not the available—fund; only income from the investment of royalties was to go into the available fund, from which the legislature could make expenditures. In the American Road Company case, Moody proved huge losses by the state on fraudulent road contracts and got a $600,000 judgment and cancellation of the firm's right to do business in Texas. Moody recovered on other contracts made by a Highway Commission which ignored competitive bidding and was influenced by the governor's husband, who sat with the commission during its deliberations. Moody ruled that the bill restoring the impeached Jim Ferguson's political rights was unconstitutional. Sam Acheson wrote:

> Scarcely had the defeat of Butte been accomplished when internal dissensions broke out in the new administration at Austin; the young, red-headed Attorney-General, Dan Moody, who had been elected on the same ticket by a much larger majority than the Governor herself, soon broke with the man who now exercised great power by virtue of his wife's office and title.

In 1926 Moody married Mildred Paxton, of Abilene, and their wedding trip was a campaign tour. Seeking to succeed Mrs. Ferguson, Moody attacked her husband as the "proxy governor" who controlled the textbook commission and was on the payroll of a railroad. He charged that the *Ferguson Forum* employed a member of the textbook commission and accepted advertising from corporations interested in pending legislation. Jim Ferguson said "This upstart" or "young spud" had "nothing to recommend him save a lipstick, a new wife, and a big head," and charged him with lack of intelligence because of his low grades in law school. Moody answered: "I have held three public offices in this state, and I have never been haled before the bar of any court of justice for misconduct in any of them. I am grateful that no decree of any high court of impeachment forbids the candidacy I am now presenting. . . ."

Angered by Moody's charges, Mrs. Ferguson told a Sulphur Springs audience of 7,000 people that she would resign as governor if Moody led by a single vote in the July 24 primary if he promised to quit as attorney general if she had a lead of 25,000 ballots. That evening, in San Antonio, Moody accepted; public offices should not be gambled, he said, but if he could rid the state of the Fergusons six months early, the means was justified. Candidate Lynch Davidson claimed his opponents had reduced the race to the stature of a crap game. The results were: Moody, 409,732; Ferguson, 283,482; Davidson, 122,449; O. F. Zimmerman, 2,962; Mrs. Edith Wilmans, 1,580; and Mrs. Kate Johnston, 1,029.

Since Moody was 1,770 votes short of a majority, a runoff would be necessary unless Mrs. Ferguson kept her bargain. For two weeks she was silent. More than two-thirds of the county conventions demanded her promised resignation, but she stayed in the race. Moody won, 495,723 to 270,595. At 33 he became Texas' youngest chief executive at a ceremony attended by six former governors.

The legislature adopted about 50% of the reforms Moody suggested. He made some good administrative appointments. The new Highway Commission was operating

Governor and Mrs. Moody hosted former president Calvin Coolidge and Mrs. Coolidge in San Antonio in March of 1930.

efficiently. Public schools were improved; the academic year was lengthened to an average of six months, annual salaries were raised to $759.00, and the cost of textbooks was reduced from $1.57 to $1.09 per student. Moody was a national figure, and there was talk of a vice presidential nomination, especially after the 1928 Democratic National Convention was scheduled for Houston, but Moody was interested only in another term as governor. His main opponent, Louis Wardlaw, of Fort Worth, a Ferguson friend apparently short on issues, accused Moody of sponsoring a geography textbook describing West Texas a sparsely-inhabited desert. (The book had been adopted years before Moody took office.) With 442,080 votes to Wardlaw's 245,508, William E. Hawkins' 32,076, and Mrs. Edith Wilmans' 18,237, Moody won the nomination without a runoff. That November the Republican Herbert Hoover barely defeated Alfred E. Smith—by 28,023 of 706,049 ballots cast—while Moody bested his Republican opponent by a margin of four to one.

Once more Moody's suggested reforms were partially accepted by the legislature, although he called five special sessions. Jim Ferguson had filed suit to nullify his impeachment disqualification; when the court held against him, Ferguson announced his wife's candidacy. Ross Sterling, a Houston oil millionaire and chairman of the Highway Commission, was her main opponent. It was not certain that Sterling's entry would keep his friend, Moody, from attempting an unprecedented third term, for Moody believed a rich man could not win, and he did not want the Fergusons back in office. But Moody was heavily in debt because of the $4,000-a-year salary, so he removed himself from the race, which included Jim Ferguson, "running behind his wife's petticoats," and Earle B. Mayfield, "neither of whom should hold public office." With Moody's help Sterling was elected. Upon leaving office Moody commented, "Well, the job is done. If it was not a good job, it is too late now."

Moody became a spectacularly successful lawyer. He assisted Sterling, in 1932, but the depression and the Fergusons were too much; a South Texas editor wrote: "It would be better to let the country go back to the Indians rather than put Jim back in the governor's chair." Ferguson had promised to "be on hand to pick up chips, bring in the wood, and carry water for Mama."

In 1942 Moody attempted to unseat Senator W. Lee O'Daniel. Unfortunately, former governor James V. Allred announced on the same day—O'Daniel called them "the Gold Dust Twins"—and they cancelled each other out. O'Daniel barely beat Allred in a runoff.

Moody returned to politics to oppose Franklin Roosevelt's fourth term. Anti-Roosevelt delegates to the 1944 Democratic State Convention elected him chairman. These "Texas Regulars" were offered seats at the national convention—although three-fourths refused and departed—with the pro-Roosevelt delegation; each delegate was to have half a vote. Moody seconded the presidential nomination of Senator Harry Byrd, of Virginia. In the balloting Moody cast twelve of his faction's votes for Roosevelt and twelve for Byrd; the other half of the delegation cast 24 for Roosevelt. For Vice President, Moody gave 21 for Harry Truman and three for Henry Wallace, and the rest of the delegation gave Wallace its 24 votes. Before the voting was closed, the factions cast 48 votes for Truman. Moody supported Eisenhower twice and helped Richard Nixon in 1960.

Dan Moody died in Austin on May 22, 1966.

Governor Moody and his children pose on the porch of the Mansion.

Ross Sterling Was a Highway Builder

Ross Shaw Sterling, named for Governor Ross, was born at Anahuac on February 11, 1875, the eighth of twelve children. The death of his mother when he was thirteen years old ended his meager education. He was a hard worker on the farm and in his father's store. He weighed 265 pounds and could carry a 200-pound sack of feed under each arm.

In 1898 Sterling married Maud Gage, who fished off a pier in front of their mansion and ran—and won—footraces with the neighborhood children when her husband was a millionaire. In 1903 he opened a feed store at Sour Lake which sold supplies to oil field operators. He expanded, bought out competitors, and repeated the process at Saratoga, Humble, and Dayton. Moving to Houston he entered the lumber business and acquired four banks.

Sterling bought an interest in two producing wells in the Humble field, and he and some friends chartered the Humble Oil Company in February, 1911. Sterling was the president. In the early twenties Sterling merged the *Houston Dispatch* and the *Houston Post* and hired W. P. Hobby to manage the *Post-Dispatch*, which was appalled by Jim Ferguson's manipulation of the Highway Commission and supported Dan Moody's effort to unseat Mrs. Ferguson. Moody made Sterling chairman of the Highway Commission; Sterling planned a system of hard-surface roads and reorganized the Highway Department. When his plan for financing state highways was not accepted, he announced for governor, despite predictions that a millionaire could not be elected. Sterling proposed a huge bond issue—funded by gasoline taxes—to finance highway building and reimburse counties for past expenditures on roads that would be part of the state system. The bond proceeds would enable counties to redeem bonds they had issued for road building, which were paid from property taxes. Sterling went into the runoff trailing Mrs. Ferguson, but with the help of Moody—who regularly stated that Jim Ferguson, the actual governor, could not be trusted—Sterling won the Democratic nomination, 473,371, to 384,402.

Sterling took office in January, 1931; it was a time of drouth and depression, which were reasons why he had only a single term. Petroleum was another major problem. Too much oil was being produced before the East Texas field—the greatest of them all—came in. Oil had dropped from $1 to 10¢ a barrel when a court held, in July, that the Railroad Commission could not impose proration since restrictions on production affected only economic—not physical—waste. (Experts had testified that unrestricted production depleted the gas needed to bring oil to the surface, which resulted in physical waste.) In August, Governor Bill Murray declared martial law and shut down Oklahoma fields until the price of crude returned to $1 a barrel. An East Texas Chamber of Commerce petition—with 1,200 names—requested that production be stopped, and on August 17 Sterling sent troops into the East Texas field, which was yielding a million barrels a day. General Jacob Wolters took 99 officers and 1,104 enlisted men to Kilgore to control about 1,600 wells. James Clark and Michael T. Halbouty, in their superb book, *The Last Boom*, noted that Sterling had not ordered

Ross Sterling, the thirty-first governor, served from January 20, 1931 to January 17, 1933.

drilling stopped, consequently, prospecting for new wells went on while production was halted. Whereas Murray had simply declared each well to be at the center of a martial law area and sent in troops, without explanation, Sterling was slow and indecisive. Furthermore, those believing proration to be a scheme of the great oil companies could offer as evidence the fact that General Wolters was Texaco's general counsel and his aide was a Gulf official.

Production, limited to 400,000 barrels a day, resumed in September. The soldiers kept the wells within the fixed allowable and tried to cut off the "hot oil" pumped and spirited out of the field. The troops were withdrawn in March, 1932, after the United States Supreme Court decided martial law had not been justified. Sterling's action had aided the conservation movement in a difficult time.

Sterling and Murray were also involved in a controversy over the three free bridges recently built on Red River. Owners of the toll bridges near Gainesville and Denison got an injunction to keep them closed. Murray, contending that Oklahoma owned both banks of Red River and both ends of the bridges, decided to open them. When Sterling sent Rangers to enforce the injunction, on July 24, 1931, Murray declared martial law around the bridges and had the Oklahoma National Guard open them to traffic. (Earlier Murray had had the north bank approaches to the toll bridges plowed up.)

Sterling's net worth was about $50 million when he took office, but he lost almost everything because of the depression and inability to devote time to his own business; even so, he sought reelection to keep the Fergusons out of government. Although his advisors urged an early and vigorous canvass, Sterling did not begin his campaign until one month before election day. Mrs. Ferguson won the runoff by 477,699 to 473,941 votes. Sterling, convinced that his defeat was due to fraud, assisted the Republican nominee in the general election and did not attend Mrs. Ferguson's inauguration. Sterling said, "When I became Governor, I was well-to-do, and now I return to the ranks of the poor from which I sprung." He amassed a new fortune and was known for his philanthropy when he died in Fort Worth on March 25, 1949.

Ross Sterling, inaugurated at a difficult time, takes the oath of office as governor.

Jimmy Allred Hosted the Centennial

Renne and Mary Allred, of Bowie, Montague County, had five sons, all of whom became lawyers: Oran was Stephens County Attorney; Ben and Jimmy were each district attorney at Wichita Falls; Raymond was the district attorney in Wheeler County; and Renne was the district judge for Gregg and Rusk counties.

James V. Allred was born March 29, 1899, near Bowie. His first job, washing soft drink bottles, paid 25¢ a day. He shined shoes and sold newspapers, attended Rice for awhile, and entered a Bowie business college. After serving in the Navy, Allred worked for a Wichita Falls law firm; then, on $1,000 borrowed from his brother, Oran, he attended Cumberland University Law School.

Allred married Jo Betsy Miller, and their third son, Sam Houston Allred, was born in the Governor's Mansion in the room which was also Temple Houston's birthplace. Appointed district attorney by Governor Neff in 1923, Allred fought the Ku Klux Klan.

After one unsuccessful attempt, Allred became attorney general in 1930. When he sought the governorship in 1934, his opponents were Tom Hunter, a Wichita Falls oilman; Charles McDonald, a Wichita Falls lawyer; Clint Small, of Amarillo; Lieutenant Governor Edgar Witt, of Waco; and Dallas lawyer Maury Hughes. Farmer Edward Russell, of Detroit, withdrew before the election. Not since 1912 had there been an election in which no Ferguson was a candidate. Allred campaigned against the lobbies, promised more equitable taxation, and—although he was a prohibitionist—urged an election on repeal of the prohibition amendment to the Texas constitution.

The *Dallas News* observed:

> Evangelism and the stage definitely were the losers when James V. Allred contributed his talents to the law and to politics. Master alike of pantomime and the spoken word there comes a time in the Allred campaign address when some of his hearers are transported back to the brush arbors of camp meetings and await the call for mourners. . . . James V. Allred is a superlative specimen of a common American phenomenon; the small town boy whose talents harnessed to energy and ambition scaled heights of achievements. . . . The Allred technique in politics is peculiarly individualistic and a little paradoxical. His very presence exudes the spirit of friendliness and yet he probably is as reserved in his intimate fellowship with men as was Pat M. Neff. . . .

Farrell and Silverthorne wrote of his unsuccessful attempt to be elected attorney general in 1926: "He was accused of being a West Texan, too young for state office, and a bachelor. He replied that his birth occurred in West Texas because his mother was there at the time, he was growing older, and was working toward ending his bachelorhood."

Texans appreciated Allred's combativeness. He said of some critics, "If you think I haven't got their number then you think I'm lazier than I am." And when General Jacob Wolters said he would resign rather than salute "that young whipper-snapper"

James V. Allred, the thirty-third governor, served from January 15, 1935 to January 17, 1939.

Allred declared "if he doesn't resign, I'll see that a courtmartial is convened and have him reduced to the rank of buck private." The vote was split so many ways, Allred was forced into an all-Wichita Falls runoff; in the second primary Allred received 499,343 votes to Hunter's 456,106, and in November he defeated Republican D. E. Waggoner easily.

On his inauguration day the *Dallas News* noted, "Today out go the Fergusons, from office forever, it is to be hoped." The Fergusons had almost destroyed the Rangers by appointing incompetents and giving some 2,000 "special" commissions to friends. Allred called captains Tom Hickman, J. W. McCormick, and Frank Hamer out of retirement to rehabilitate the Ranger force.

Allred began cultivating the good will of Mexico. Sarah T. Hughes became the state's first woman district judge. (In 1963 she administered the presidential oath to Lyndon Johnson after John Kennedy's death.) He set up an old-age assistance program; amounts were small, but 50,000 Texans began receiving payments on July 1, 1936. Allred created parole and pardoning machinery to correct the abuses of the Ferguson years. In the election he had advocated, statewide prohibition was repealed.

In 1936, Allred faced Tom Hunter again. F. W. Fischer, a Tyler lawyer, Roy Sanderford, of Belton, and Pierce P. Brooks, of Dallas, were also in the race, but it was an Allred year. He hosted the centennial celebration, the Jaycees honored him as the nation's outstanding young man, and he nominated Vice President John Nance Garner at the Democratic National Convention. When Lyndon Johnson ran for Congress, in a 1937 special election occasioned by the death of James P. Buchanan, Allred introduced Johnson to President Roosevelt, who was fishing in the Gulf. Johnson returned to Washington on the President's special train. The governor had asked for legislation prohibiting race track betting, and in a 1937 special session such a statute was passed.

Allred became judge of the new Southern District of Texas, in 1939, but he resigned to run against Senator W. Lee O'Daniel in 1942. In the special election made necessary by Senator Morris Sheppard's death, O'Daniel had barely beaten young Congressman Lyndon Johnson. This time O'Daniel defeated both Allred and Dan Moody. Through the efforts of Senator Lyndon B. Johnson, Allred was appointed to the federal bench by President Harry S. Truman in 1949. He died September 24, 1959, while holding court at Laredo. Mrs. Allred returned to Wichita Falls and taught in City View Elementary School until she reached retirement age.

Austin-Travis County Collection, Austin Public Library

Governor Allred tries out his Texas Centennial boots.

Governor Allred, promoting the Centennial, is joined by Hollywood stars Ginger Rogers and John Boles.

James V. Allred delivers his address after being sworn in for a second term.

W. Lee O'Daniel Changed Texas Politics

Wilbert Lee O'Daniel, born March 11, 1890, at Malta, Ohio, was still an infant when his father, a Union veteran, was killed in an industrial accident. His mother remarried, and the family moved to a Kansas tenant farm when O'Daniel was four years old. After high school graduation he attended a Hutchinson, Kansas, business college, worked for some milling companies, and owned a flour mill by the time he was 26. He married Merle Butcher, of Hutchinson.

O'Daniel came to Fort Worth, in 1925, as sales manager of the Burrus Mill and Elevator Company. When unemployed musicians Bob Wills, Herman Arnspiger, and Milton Brown asked that Burrus sponsor them on the radio, O'Daniel consented. They called themselves the Light Crust Doughboys. After two weeks on KFJZ, whose studio was a back room in Meacham's Department Store, whose transmitter sat on top of a telephone pole at the edge of town, and which had a range of about fifteen miles, O'Daniel cancelled; he did not like the kind of music they played. After waiting two or three days in his reception room, Bob Wills got to see O'Daniel. Finally, O'Daniel promised to sponsor a daily radio program and pay each musician $7.50 a week, but everyone had to work forty hours weekly at the flour mill. Arnspiger recalled: "Our hands were so sore and stiff you couldn't note a guitar or play a fiddle."

The band went on the air in January, 1931, and sold lots of Light Crust Flour. Because of their immediate popularity O'Daniel raised them to $15 a week and excused them from driving trucks and loading flour, but they still had to practice their music at the mill forty hours a week. O'Daniel disdained what he termed their "hillbilly music" until the day Wills invited him to say a few words on the radio. From then on O'Daniel was part of the daily program. He succeeded Truett Kimsey as the announcer. They moved to the more powerful WBAP to reach a larger audience. When their salaries reached $25 a week, O'Daniel demanded that the band stop playing dances. Loss of the extra income caused the others to quit, and finally Wills left in 1933. O'Daniel hired other musicians and sued Wills for advertising that his band was formerly the Light Crust Doughboys, but the judges—O'Daniel went all the way to the United States Supreme Court—held that Wills had only told the truth. O'Daniel persuaded radio staton WKY, in Oklahoma City, to fire Wills, and attempted, without success, to get Tulsa's KVOO to discharge him and his band. O'Daniel attracted a huge following; he wrote such songs as "Beautiful Texas" and poetry with religious overtones, which he read on the midday program.

When O'Daniel bought his own company, in 1935, and began selling Hillbilly Flour, the band became the Hillbilly Boys. A million people heard them each day. From time to time O'Daniel mentioned over the air that he had been urged to run for governor. On Palm Sunday, he asked his listeners' advice and received 50,000 requests to make the race. O'Daniel announced that his platform would be the Ten Commandments and a $30-a-month pension for everyone over 65. Using the slogan, "Less Johnson grass and politicians and more smokestacks and business men," he expected the audience to finance him:

W. Lee O'Daniel, the thirty-fourth governor, took office January 17, 1939 and resigned to enter the United States Senate on August 4, 1941.

159

> If you want me to run the race on a bicycle, while the other candidates have high-powered racing cars, that is up to you. . . . I say to you in all sincerity. . .you had better take that old rocking chair down and mortgage it and spend the money in the manner you think best to get your pension. . . . We have not one dollar in our campaign fund.

O'Daniel revolutionized campaign styles by taking the band along on his speaking engagements. He offered Texans entertainment with their politics. His attractive children, Pat, Mike and Molly, circulated through the crowds with miniature flour barrels accepting contributions. The largest crowds in Texas political history turned out to hear "Pappy" O'Daniel, whose nickname came from the line regularly used on the radio show: "Please pass the biscuits, Pappy." From then on candidates felt obliged to offer more than speeches. For example, Jerry Sadler, challenging O'Daniel, in 1940, was accompanied by Sadler's Cowboy Stringsters and Texas A &M's All-American fullback, Jarring John Kimbrough. Such attempts were always inadequate, for O'Daniel offered a voice and music that voters had heard on the radio for years, while his competitors were merely hopeful candidates with musicians.

O'Daniel beat Ernest O. Thompson, of Amarillo, and eleven others without a runoff, carrying 231 of the 254 counties. His promises could not possibly be kept. There were no funds for a $30-a-month pension; he could not get rid of the poll tax; and he could not abolish the death penalty. O'Daniel's regular attacks on "professional politicians" reflected a self-righteousness that alienated legislators whose help was needed to keep his pledges. (One of his defeated opponents, Attorney General William McCraw, wrote a book, *Professional Politicians*, about the most revered figures in Texas public life—Houston, Lamar, Lubbock, Hogg and Reagan. McCraw quoted Pat Neff's inaugural address: "Politics is not a game. It is the science of public service. It furnishes a broad field of noble endeavor. In this realm of labor are finally won the things that make a people great and good.")

O'Daniel's inauguration took place in the University of Texas football stadium and lasted five hours; nearly 10,000 children and bands from forty high schools and colleges took part in the program. O'Daniel's children attended the state university and participated in the Sunday morning radio broadcasts from the Mansion. When Molly married Jack Wrather, the governor invited his radio audience; about 25,000 Texans came to Austin and heard the ceremony over loudspeakers on the grounds of the Mansion.

Responding to adverse newspaper coverage, in his 1940 reelection the governor started the *W. Lee O'Daniel News*, which cost 25¢ for a four-month subscription. (Profits, the governor promised, would go to the Red Cross.) O'Daniel charged that "No recent governor has been so unfairly dealt with as the press has dealt with me." Lynn Landrum, of the *Dallas News* wrote:

> In the vague, burbling, tentative logic that characterizes our governor, the large objective is to have more O'Daniel in print. News is something about O'Daniel. Accurate news is something complimentary of O'Daniel. Reliable news is something complimentary of O'Daniel by O'Daniel himself. . . .

In 1940 the Fergusons were back; Mrs. Ferguson recommended third terms for herself and Franklin Roosevelt, and Mr. Ferguson called O'Daniel "a misplaced musician who crooned his way into the governor's office and has been giving the people of Texas a song and dance ever since. . . ." Ernest O. Thompson, O'Daniel's

160

A seller of pennants and badges does a brisk business at O'Daniel's second inaugural.

principal opponent, explained his small crowd at Greenville by saying,

> I don't yodel. . . . O'Daniel was elected by accident. He started out to run for governor to advertise his flour business. People laughed and voted for him and the first thing they knew he was elected governor. I will admit he fooled me. I spent all my time last election fighting Bill McCraw of Dallas. Then O'Daniel passed me in a cloud of flour dust like a freight train passing a tramp.

Again O'Daniel was nominated without a runoff, drawing 645,646 votes to Thompson's 256,923, Harry Hines' 119,121, Mrs. Ferguson's 100,578, Jerry Sadler's 61,396, Cyclone Davis' 3,623 and R. P. Condron's 2,003. O'Daniel lost only nine of 254 counties.

A few months after O'Daniel's second inauguration, Senator Morris Sheppard died. To serve pending a special election, the governor appointed Sam Houston's son, 87-year-old Andrew Jackson Houston, who died about three weeks after reaching Washington. In that 1941 election, O'Daniel defeated Congressman Lyndon Johnson and about two dozen others. Seeking reelection, in 1942, Senator O'Daniel led former governors Allred and Moody but was forced into a runoff, which he won by 18,000 of almost 900,000 cast. After an undistinguished Senate term, O'Daniel ran an insurance company in Dallas, where he died on May 11, 1969. Mrs. O'Daniel died in 1972.

O'Daniel shot a buffalo for the barbecue celebrating his inauguration.

Mr. Kraft, of the Kraft Cheese family, visited O'Daniel's radio broadcast in March, 1940. One of the governor's sons is second from the left, playing the fiddle, and the other stands between Kraft and O'Daniel, holding a banjo.

O'Daniel appointed Andrew Jackson Houston to the United States Senate on San Jacinto Day, 1941. The aged Houston and his daughters stand between Mrs. O'Daniel and the governor.

"Calculating Coke" Was the Wartime Governor

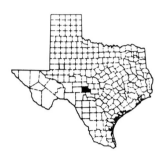

Coke Robert Stevenson—named for Governor Richard Coke—was the first man to hold Texas' three highest offices and probably the only one to carry all 254 counties in a contested primary. Born in Mason County, on March 20, 1888, he grew up in Kimble County. He spent only 22 months in school; most of his education was received from his parents. (Mr. Stevenson was a teacher at Little Saline, Bear Creek, and Pegleg schools.) Stevenson, at age ten, earned a dollar a week working for a rancher, and at sixteen he was hauling freight between Junction and the railhead at Brady, 75 miles away; the round-trip took a week. Beginning as janitor of Junction's new First State Bank, he was cashier by his 21st birthday. Because of limited finances, when he and Fay Wright married, in 1912, they wrecked two old houses, and, in their spare time, built a home from the lumber.

In the next few years Stevenson bought a ranch, read law, opened Junction's first movie theater, an automobile agency, and a hardware store. Later, while president of the First National Bank, he was also the First State's attorney.

Stevenson's first venture into politics, in 1914, was as Kimble County Attorney. He prosecuted thieves who were making life hard for goat and sheep ranchers. Then, as county judge, he built badly needed roads; there was not a mile of Kimble County pavement in 1918. He had been out of office for eight years when he was elected to the legislature, in 1929. Because hill country ranchers lost heavily to predators, bounties were offered on wolves shot on the Edwards Plateau. Hunters began bringing wolves from the other parts of Texas; in one county a wolf bootlegger was paid $2,000 for imported animals. Stevenson offered an amendment to the bounty law making it a crime to take a wolf across a county line. Twice he was elected speaker of the House, an honor without precedent in modern times. He won a runoff with Pierce Brooks, of Dallas, 446,441 to 400,444, to become lieutenant governor, as W. Lee O'Daniel and his band captured the governorship.

When Senator Morris Sheppard died suddenly, O'Daniel appointed Andrew Jackson Houston, the son of the first Texas senator, to the vacancy. In the June, 1941, special election, O'Daniel defeated Lyndon Johnson and several other strong candidates by only 1,311 ballots out of 575,879 cast. Stevenson succeeded O'Daniel in August, 1941, only weeks before the Japanese attack on Pearl Harbor. Mrs. Stevenson attended her husband's inaugural on a stretcher; she died January 3, 1942.

During World War II, 1,250,000 servicemen trained in the state, and 750,000 Texans were in the armed forces. In 1942 Hal Collins, of the Crazy Water Crystals radio program, ran for governor. Collins campaigned with his friend, Senator O'Daniel, who was seeking reelection, but association with O'Daniel did not save Collins from a sound thrashing by Stevenson. His 1944 performance was even more spectacular; Stevenson's eight opponents polled only 16% of the ballots.

In the year following the end of his term, Stevenson and Lyndon Johnson—battling for the Senate seat being vacated by O'Daniel—made it into a runoff, where they staged the closest race in Texas history. On September 2, Stevenson was 249 votes

Coke Stevenson, the thirty-fifth governor, served from August 4, 1941 to January 21, 1947.

ahead, with 253 of 254 counties reporting, but before the official canvass, eleven days later, Jim Wells County officials claimed that Box 13, in Alice, had been erroneously reported; the corrected return showed an additional 202 votes for Johnson and one for Stevenson. This provided an 87-vote margin for Johnson: 494,191 to 494,104. Local boss George Parr had thrown the county to Johnson out of pique for Stevenson's failure to appoint a Parr man to a job.

In 1954 Stevenson married the district clerk at Junction, Mrs. Marguerite King Heap, whose husband had died in the war. The former Democratic governor supported Republicans Eisenhower and Nixon. He died in a San Angelo hospital on June 28, 1975, and was buried on his Kimble County Ranch.

Coke Stevenson was one of the best vote-getters in Texas politics.

Beauford Jester Died in Office

Beauford Halbert Jester, born January 12, 1893, at Corsicana, was the son of Lieutenant Governor George T. Jester, and the great grandson of Hampton McKinney, who built the first house in Corsicana, on what is now the courthouse square. After graduating from the University of Texas he entered Harvard Law School but joined the Army when the United States declared war on Germany. He attended the First Officers' Training Corp, at Leon Springs. As a 90th Division captain he took part in several battles and spent six months on occupation duty in Germany. Jester received his law degree from the University of Texas in 1920 and married Mabel Buchanan the next year. He practiced law in Corsicana and was a regent of the state university. He was a very able member of the Railroad Commission.

Jester became governor in perhaps the most vicious—and ridiculous—campaign in Texas history. Charges were made which have not been surpassed in irresponsibility and inanity. Some of the heat was due to the state university's involvement. The candidacy of Homer Rainey, a former president of the University of Texas, precipitated passionate fights over such issues as the suitability of John Dos Passos' *U.S.A.* as assigned reading for college students. Conservative regents appointed by O'Daniel and Stevenson had sought the dismissal of professors and otherwise interfered with administration of the university. In the Dos Passos controversy the faculty gave President Rainey a vote of confidence, the regents fired Rainey, and the Southern Association of Colleges and Secondary Schools and the American Association of University Professors expressed their disapproval of the regents.

The fourteen candidates in the 1946 gubernatorial primary included Attorney General Grover Sellers, Lieutenant Governor John Lee Smith, former railroad commissioner Jerry Sadler, and Caso March, of Waco. While Rainey argued for economic growth and financial independence from the East, some of his opponents whipped to death the university controversy. Smith called *U.S.A.* "one of the basest books ever written," and March declared it "a filthy volume wholly unfit to be offered our young people." The *Dallas News* reported how women wept after Sadler told of a University of Texas professor ridiculing Christian prayer at a time when mothers were awaiting their sons' safe return from the war. Hal Collins, assisting Smith, asked a rally, "If Joe Stalin were voting in Texas, who would he vote for?" Members of his western band shouted "Rainey." At "for men only" rallies, Sellers read aloud parts of *U.S.A.* and warned that such books would destroy civilization.

In the first primary Jester had 443,804 votes and Homer P. Rainey, 291,282, Grover Sellers' 162,431, Jerry Sadler, 103,120, and John Lee Smith 102,941. In the runoff Jester's margin was two to one over Rainey. He was reelected without a runoff in 1948.

Jester died on July 11, 1948, aboard a Pullman on his way to a speaking engagement in Galveston. A porter in Houston, who attempted to wake him, discovered that he had died during the night, apparently of a heart attack.

Beauford Jester, the thirty-sixth governor, was inaugurated January 21, 1947. He died July 11, 1949.

Allan Shivers Served the Longest Time

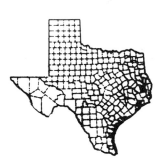

On July 11, 1949, Robert Allan Shivers succeeded Beauford Jester, who was the only Texas governor to die in office. After completing Jester's term Shivers won three elections and served a record 7½ years as governor. Born October 5, 1907, in Lufkin, Shivers grew up at Woodville, where his father was the county judge. He worked for the *Tyler County Messenger* and jerked sodas. His family moved when he was sixteen, and he graduated from Port Arthur High School in 1924. He dropped out of college to work in the railroad shops at Port Arthur, then returned to be president of the student body and clerk at the J. C. Penney store in Austin. After receiving the B.A. from the University of Texas, Shivers passed the bar examination before graduation from law school.

At 26 Shivers was elected to the state Senate as James V. Allred became governor. When "Allred got the idea that he was entitled to cast my vote in the Senate because he had appointed my father district judge," Shivers parted company with the governor. Allred had demanded Shivers' support in ending pari-mutuel betting.

In 1937 Shivers married Marialice Shary, whose father, a major entrepreneur in the lower Rio Grande Valley, had pioneered the citrus industry. The wedding took place in the great mansion—set in an 800-acre citrus orchard—at Sharyland, near Mission. Sam Kinch and Stuart Long wrote that once the entire legislature was invited there, and the living room was large enough to seat everyone.

In World War II Major Shivers served overseas in military government; upon his return he was the oldest member of the state Senate in point of service. Shivers' colleagues chose him to succeed Lieutenant Governor John Lee Smith. His opponents were Joe Winfree and Boyce House. Shivers defeated newspaperman House in a runoff as Beauford Jester won the governorship.

Lieutenant Governor Shivers proposed annual legislative sessions and four-year terms for elected officials. Believing the state had to serve her people more fully in order to slow the growth of the federal government, Shivers planned to run for governor when Jester concluded his second term.

Jester—bound for Galveston by train—was found dead in his Pullman berth on July 12, 1948, and the 41-year-old Shivers was sworn in as governor at the Woodville farm where his widowed great-grandmother had settled her family more than a century before. In 1950 he defeated Caso March and five others to retain the office.

The struggle with the federal government over ownership of the marginal seas—the "tidelands"—was growing bitter. Congressional attempts to quitclaim the disputed territories to the states were frustrated by President Truman's veto. In 1952 the Republican nominee, Dwight Eisenhower, promised to deed the "tidelands" to the states; however, the Democrat Adlai Stevenson refused. Shivers, a Democratic governor, then assumed leadership of Eisenhower's successful effort in Texas. The law in 1952 permitted a candidate to be listed on the ballot as the nominee of more than one party; Shivers received 375,547 votes as a Democrat and 468,319 as a Republican.

When he sought reelection, in 1954, Shivers had difficulty because of third-term

Allan Shivers, the thirty-seventh governor, finished Jester's term. He served from July 11, 1949 to January 15, 1957.

resistance, but most of the bitterness shown him resulted from his aid to the Republicans. He achieved a slight lead over his main opponent, Ralph Yarborough, in the first primary, 668,913 to 645,994. (Arlon B. (Cyclone) Davis and another minor candidate got 31,000 votes.) Shivers prevailed by 92,000 votes in the runoff. In 1956 he again helped Eisenhower defeat Stevenson.

On the day Price Daniel was inaugurated, Allan Shivers took possession of Woodlawn, the former Austin home of Governor E. M. Pease. Niles Graham, Pease's grandson, turned the old mansion over to the new owner exactly 100 years after his ancestor left office and moved from the Governor's Mansion—where Pease had been the first occupant—to Woodlawn, which was then four years old.

Allan Shivers was the first governor elected to three terms.

Price Daniel Ran for a Fourth Term

Marion Price Daniel, whose ancestors had settled in Liberty County in 1824, was born in Dayton, on October 10, 1910. After graduating from a Fort Worth high school and working for the *Fort Worth Star-Telegram*, he graduated from Baylor in 1931 while reporting for the *Waco News-Tribune*. His Baylor law degree was conferred the following year, and he opened a law office at Liberty. Daniel became a legislator in 1938, about the time he began publishing the *Liberty Vindicator* and the *Anahuac Progress*. An opponent of W. Lee O'Daniel's transactions tax, he was chosen speaker of the House.

In 1943 Daniel joined the Army as a private. He was discharged as a captain just before his 1946 election as attorney general. His reelection was by a vote of 1,231,881—until then the largest total in a Texas election. Daniel won a third term; his popularity was partially due to his fight in behalf of Texas' claim to the marginal seas. After the United States Supreme Court, in 1950, held that the federal government owned the oil beneath the so-called "tidelands," bills granting those submerged areas to the states were vetoed by President Harry Truman.

Daniel announced, in 1952, for the seat of the aged Senator Tom Connally and defeated East Texas Congressman Lindley Beckworth for the nomination. Although running as a Democrat, he assisted Republican nominee Dwight Eisenhower; he explained that he hoped to influence Eisenhower on the tidelands. Senator Daniel resigned to become governor of Texas in January, 1957. In the first primary he polled 628,914 votes to Ralph Yarborough's 463,416, W. Lee O'Daniel's 347,757, and J. Evetts Haley's 88,772; but he barely survived the runoff with Ralph Yarborough, 698,001 to 694,830. The general election was no contest, although W. Lee O'Daniel drew a surprising 110,234 write-in votes. Daniel was easily reelected over Henry B. Gonzalez, of San Antonio, and W. Lee O'Daniel, who ran almost as well as Gonzalez. Daniel's attempt at a fourth term was frustrated by John Connally. He won a place on the Texas Supreme Court in 1972.

Daniel married Jean Houston Baldwin, a great-great granddaughter of Sam Houston. (She presided over the Mansion exactly a century after Margaret Houston lived there. During World War II she gave birth to her third child, Houston, at Lexington, Virginia, in the county where Sam Houston was born.) Price Daniel, Jr. was speaker of the House and chairman of the 1974 Constitutional Convention; his wife is a great granddaughter of Governor Tom Campbell.

Price Daniel, the thirty-eighth governor, served from January 15, 1957 to January 15, 1963.

John Connally Was Shot at the Triple Underpass

John Bowden Connally Jr., born February 27, 1917, in Wilson County, said, "Our small ranch was a living for a large family, and it took long, hard hours of work by every member of my family to make ends meet. We plowed behind a mule, got our water from a hand-pump, studied by kerosene light. . . ." The family moved to San Antonio when Connally was in the sixth grade, but he graduated from Floresville High School. At the state university he managed the successful campaign of J. J. Pickle—now the Austin congressman—for student body president. In the following year Pickle was the manager as Connally won the office. Connally's part-time jobs included dishwasher and disc jockey.

In 1939 he went to work for Congressman Lyndon Johnson, who was the best man when Connally married Idanell Brill. He had already been admitted to the bar when he got his law degree in 1941. Soon after Pearl Harbor he went on active duty with the Navy and was discharged as a lieutenant commander. After the war Connally helped organize radio station KVET, which he served as president. Jake Pickle was the business manager.

Connally managed Lyndon Johnson's 1948 Senate campaign and became the senator's administrative assistant. Although he returned to Texas to practice law, in Austin and then Fort Worth—where he was counsel to oilman Sid Richardson—Connally helped in Johnson's various races. Connally became one of three executors of the Sid Richardson estate, which had assets of perhaps a billion dollars.

Connally assisted in Johnson's unsuccessful bid for the 1960 presidential nomination. Finally Lyndon Johnson accepted second place on the Kennedy ticket, and soon after his inauguration, John Kennedy made Connally Secretary of the Navy. The appointment provoked objections because the Navy was the world's largest purchaser of oil, but the Senate—except for Wisconsin's Proxmire—saw no conflict of interest. About a year later Connally became a candidate for governor. His first campaign speech was at the Hotel Brownwood, which is now a Howard Payne University dormitory, Sid Richardson Hall. He led in the first primary with 431,498 votes to Don Yarborough's 317,986 and Price Daniel's 248,524. In the runoff Connally beat Yarborough, 565,174 to 538,924. The general election was, until then, the most successful Republican effort in Texas history; Jack Cox drew 715,025 votes to Connally's 847,038. (Two years before, Cox, as a Democrat, had given Price Daniel stiff competition.)

The victory almost cost Connally's life, for it was his function as governor to serve as President John F. Kennedy's host. In Dallas, on November 22, 1963, Governor and Mrs. Connally were occupying the jump seats in front of the President as his limousine passed through downtown Dallas. Of John Kennedy, Connally wrote:

> He was watching the crowds, waving at them steadily with stiff forearm, his right hand moving only a few inches out from his face and back. It was a small movement and curiously formal but I thought, quite effective. I heard a low monotone rumble from the back and then I realized he was responding—"Thank you, thank you," over and over to

John Connally, the thirty-ninth governor, served from January 15, 1963 to January 21, 1969.

people who couldn't hear him but who could sense he was answering them, who knew that contact had been made.

As they passed the School Book Depository two shots were fired. The second one hit Connally, entering his back just left of his right shoulder blade, coming out the front of his chest, through his right wrist, and into his left thigh. As he slumped forward, Connally's right arm covered the large hole in his chest, which probably saved his life. According to Jimmy Banks, Connally said, "I don't know how much blood I lost, but they gave me two and one-half quarts. That's about one-third of the body's supply. I am a very lucky man."

It was four months before he was able to sign mail with his right hand. After three very successful terms as governor, Connally became Secretary of the Treasury in the Nixon administration on February 11, 1971. He supported Nixon in the 1972 election, then switched to the Republican party.

John Connally stands beside Anita Bryant shortly before delivering the eulogy at the funeral of President Lyndon B. Johnson.

Preston Smith Grew Up on the High Plains

The first governor from west of the 100th meridian, Preston Smith was one of thirteen children. He was born on a Williamson County tenant farm in 1912, and his education began at the one-room Mount Prospect school, where his teacher, Margaret Rabian White, recalled:

> There were Swedes and Czechs, Bohemians and Germans, and two Anglo families—the Smiths and the Carters—who sent their children to me. The Smiths were the only tenant farmers and they were the poorest.

The family moved to a Dawson County farm in 1923. After finishing the Sunset school, Smith worked in a grocery store-filling station to attend Lamesa High School. At Texas Tech he and a friend started a service station, and he ran student rooming houses. In 1934, after graduation, he married Ima Smith, of Ralls; they had met in a government class where the seating was in alphabetical order. (Ima Smith Smith's daughter, Jan, changed her name only slightly; she married a Schmid.) Smith opened, with a partner, the Tech theater. Smith said, "We couldn't pay cash for help, so we started getting Tech football players to work for us in exchange for passes." By 1944 he owned several theaters.

Smith was a legislator until 1950, when he ran third in a race for lieutenant governor; Ben Ramsey defeated Pierce Brooks in the runoff. After losing a campaign for the Senate, in 1956 Smith bested the incumbent, Kilmer Corbin. At Austin he represented farmers and West Texas, and after six years in the Senate he ran for lieutenant governor against Crawford Martin, (who was later attorney general), Speaker of the House James Turman, and senators Jarrard Secrest, of Temple, and Robert Baker, of Houston. In the 1962 election, as John Connally was denying Governor Price Daniel a fourth term, Smith trailed Turman by 70,000 votes but he won the runoff and beat Republican O. W. Hayes, 937,377 to 612,568.

Smith sought the governorship in 1968. John Connally, having completed three terms, was supporting Eugene Locke, a former deputy ambassador to Vietnam. Among Smith's twelve opponents were Uvalde rancher Dolph Briscoe, Jr.; Gordon McClendon, of Dallas and KLIF; former attorney general Waggoner Carr, of Lubbock; Pat O'Daniel, the son of W. Lee O'Daniel; former secretary of state John Hill, of Houston; Don Yarborough, a Houston lawyer who had almost beaten Connally; Alfonso Veloz, of Houston; and Johnnie Mae Hackworth, a minister from Brenham. Locke's well-financed campaign, featuring catchy jingles proclaiming that "Eugene Locke should be governor of Texas..." was effective, for he was not known to Texas voters; Locke attracted 218,712 votes, compared to the 5,000 to 22,000 of candidates equally new to Texas politics. Yarborough led with 422,823 votes, followed by Smith's 382,335, Carr's 257,202, and Briscoe's 225,610, but in the runoff Smith drew 756,909 and Yarborough got only 620,726 votes.

Preston Smith, the fortieth governor, served from January 21, 1969 to January 16, 1973.

Dolph Briscoe Won a Four-Year Term

Dolph Briscoe, Jr., born in Uvalde on April 23, 1923, graduated from the University of Texas in 1942 and married Betty Jane Slaughter, of Austin. For the next two and a half years he served in the Army, in the China-Burma-Indian theatre.

Briscoe had eight years in the legislature, never attracting an opponent after the first election. With Navasota's Senator Neveille Colson, he sponsored the farm-to-market roads which changed the lives of rural Texans. The Junior Chamber of Commerce named him an "outstanding young Texan," and he was president of the Southwestern Cattle Raisers Association in 1960-2, an office his father had held in 1932-4. (The only other father and son presidents were Robert J. and Richard Kleberg, of the King Ranch.) The elder Briscoe had failed twice in ranching; one of his ventures was a partnership with Governor Ross Sterling.

Briscoe lost his 1968 bid for the governorship; retiring incumbent John Connally was supporting Eugene Locke, and the competition included Preston Smith, the lieutenant governor, Waggoner Carr, the attorney general, John Hill, the secretary of state, and Houston attorney Don Yarborough. Briscoe wound up in fourth place and helped Smith defeat Yarborough in the second primary.

Dolph Briscoe announced in 1972 against Preston Smith, who was seeking a third term, Lieutenant Governor Ben Barnes, and Frances Farenthold. Briscoe drew 963,397 votes in the Democratic primary, leaving Governor Smith far behind—with 190,709—but was forced into a runoff with Mrs. Farenthold, who had 612,057 votes. He won but had a difficult time with the Republican Henry Grover and others, so that for the first time the governor of Texas was elected with less than a majority, 1,633,493 out of 3,409,501 ballots cast.

The constitution had been amended to provide for a four-year term when Briscoe, in 1974, won the Democratic nomination from Mrs. Farenthold and nearly doubled the vote of Republican Jim Granberry. Briscoe ranches over a million acres; according to Jimmy Banks, he owns more land and bank stock than anyone else in Texas.

Dolph Briscoe, Jr., the forty-first governor, was inaugurated January 16, 1973.

Bill Clements was the First Republican Governor in a Hundred Years

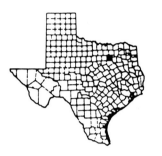

William P. Clements, Jr., born April 13, 1917 in Dallas, was the son of William Perry and Evelyn Cammack Clements. He was an all-state guard on the Highland Park football team and graduated in 1934. He had intended to go to college, but his father lost his job and Clements went to work as an oil field roughneck in South Texas. After about a year Clements was able to enroll in Southern Methodist University as an engineering student.

But the high pay of the oil fields — $150 a month — had spoiled him; roughnecks earned more than graduate engineers, so without taking a degree he left S.M.U. where later he would be chairman of the Board of Governors.

Toddie Lee Wynne made it possible for Clements and his partner, Ike LaRue, to start a drilling company. In 1947 Clements founded SEDCO, Inc., which drilled wells all over the world. By 1983 SEDCO was doing half a billion dollars worth of business annually.

Mrs. Clements, the former Rita Crocker, was born in Newton, Kansas but grew up in McCulloch County, Texas. She superintended a badly-needed renovation and restoration of the Governors Mansion. Because of the multi-million dollar project, Governor and Mrs. Clements occupied the house less than half of his term.

Clements' children are B. Gill Clements and Nancy Clements Seay.

From 1973 to 1977 Clements was Deputy Secretary of Defense in the Nixon administration. According to Robert Tomaho's *Dallas News* profile, Clements decided to seek office after Republican officials Peter O'Donnell and Walter Fleming urged him to run against Senator Ralph Yarborough. Clements had refused, but recommended that George Bush make that race. In 1977 Clements became interested in the governorship. Republican Paul Eggers, who had waged impressive campaigns against Preston Smith in 1968 and 1970, encouraged him.

It had been 104 years since a Republican was governor, and Texans did not cherish memories of E. J. Davis. In 1978 few voters thought the sixty-one-year-old political unknown had a chance. The Democratic nominee, Attorney General John Hill, had defeated the incumbent Governor Dolph Briscoe, Jr. in the primary and he was not likely to lose. In fact, Clements' margin was slender: only 16,909 ballots of 2,350,747 cast.

Clements expected to be re-elected, for Texas governors usually were given two terms. He was surprised and dismayed when Attorney General Mark White defeated him. In a heavy turnout — 3,163,807 ballots — White received 53.66%. The campaign had cost Clements $13 million, more than twice White's expenditure.

In August of 1984 Clements told a *Dallas News* interviewer, "No sir, I'll never run for office again. . . Once is enough." Nevertheless, in the 1986 Republican primary he bested three good candidates to set up a re-match with Mark White.

William P. Clements, Jr., the forty-second governor, was inaugurated January 16, 1979.

Mark White Provoked the Teachers

Mark Wells White was born in Henderson, Rusk County, March 17, 1940 to Sarah Elizabeth and Mark Wells White, Sr. He grew up in Houston and graduated from Baylor University in 1962. After receiving his law degree from Baylor in 1965 he married Linda Gale Thompson, of Irving. Their children are Mark Wells, III, Andrew, and Elizabeth Marie White.

After serving three years as an assistant attorney general White practiced in Houston until 1973, when Governor Briscoe appointed him secretary of state. He announced his candidacy for the office of attorney general in 1978. His main opponent, former Speaker of the House Price Daniel, Jr., had an outstanding record of public service. His father had been governor and senator, and his mother was a descendant of Sam Houston. Nevertheless, White captured 59% of the primary vote and had little trouble with Republican James Baker, the present Secretary of the Treasury.

White and Bill Clements took office at the same time. Very little love was lost between the two. Clements charged the attorney general with incompetence, while White called the governor "a clown" who used "smear tactics." With the assistance of thousands of teachers, White blocked Clements' re-election, 1,697,870 to 1,465,937.

White increased consumer influence with the Public Utilities Commission. He appointed more minorities and women to state boards and commissions than had any other governor. According to Dave McNeely, by February 1985 White's appointments included 921 males (75%), 307 females (25%), 917 whites (75%), 121 blacks (10%), and 190 Hispanics (15%).

White had promised better teachers' salaries without any tax increase; however, he was forced to seek more taxes. In spite of higher earnings, most teachers had been alienated. White had asked H. Ross Perot to study the public schools and make recommendations. Perot's commission discovered problems with which most classroom teachers were already familiar. The governor and legislature used the Perot findings to make changes.

Some necessary reforms were realized, but at a terrible cost. Teachers were pitted against each other in a "career ladder" program. They were forced to take an examination that cost several millions of tax dollars and was of negligible value. And teachers were inundated with paperwork that made educating the young more difficult than before.

Problems caused by cheap oil, growing unemployment, and a huge state deficit contributed to Clements' apparent lead in August 1986. But White's supporters were not overly concerned, for polls four years earlier had shown Clements with 52% of the vote on the same election day that White turned him out of office.

Mark Wells White, the forty-third governor, was inaugurated January 18, 1983.

References

Books

Acheson, Sam. *Joe Bailey, The Last Democrat.* New York: Macmillan, 1932.

Adams, Frank, ed., *Texas Democracy*, Vol. I. Austin: Democratic Historical Association, 1936.

Banks, Jimmy. *Money, Marbles and Chalk.* Austin: Texas Publishing Co., 1971.

Bartley, Ernest R. *The Tidelands Oil Controversy.* Austin: University of Texas Press, 1953.

Biographical Directory of the American Congress, 1794-1971. Washington, D.C.: U. S. Government Printing Office, 1971.

Biographical Directory of the Texas Conventions and Congresses. Austin: Book Exchange, Inc., 1941.

Brown, John Henry. *History of Texas, 1685-1892.* St. Louis: L. E. Daniell, 1893.

Candee, Marjorie Dent, ed., *Current Biography, 1956.* New York: H. W. Wilson, 1956.

Clark, James A. *The Tactful Texan: A Biography of Governor Will Hobby.* New York: Random House, 1958.

Clark, James A. and Halbouty, Michael T. *The Last Boom.* New York: Random House, 1972.

Clarke, Mary Whatley. *David G. Burnet.* Austin: Pemberton Press, 1969.

Conn, Jerry Douglas. *Preston Smith, The Making of a Texas Governor.* Austin: Pemberton Press, 1972.

Cotner, Robert C. *James Stephen Hogg.* Austin: University of Texas Press, 1959.

Crawford, Ann Fears and Keever, Jack. *John B. Connally, Portrait in Power.* Austin: Jenkins, 1973.

Current Biography, 1956.

Daniell, L. E. *Texas, The Country and Its Men.* [1916].

Daniell, L. E. *Personnel of the Texas State Government.* San Antonio: Maverick Printing House, 1892.

Day, Donald and Ullom, Harry Herbert, eds., *The Autobiography of Sam Houston.* Norman: University of Oklahoma Press, 1954.

Dixon, Sam Houston and Kemp, Louis W. *The Heroes of San Jacinto.* Houston: Anson Jones Press, 1932.

DeCordova, Jacob. *Texas: Her Resources and Her Public Men.* Philadelphia: J. B. Lippincott, 1858.

DeShields, James P. *They Sat in High Place.* San Antonio: Naylor, 1940.

Elliott, Claude. *Leathercoat, the Life History of a Texas Patriot.* San Antonio: Standard Printing, 1938.

Farrell, Mary D. and Silverthorne, Elizabeth. *First Ladies of Texas, The First 100 Years, 1836-1936.* Belton: Stillhouse-Hollow, 1976.

Fitzgerald, Hugh. *Governors I Have Known.* Austin: American-Statesman, 1927.

Friend, Llerena B. *Sam Houston, The Great Designer.* Austin: University of Texas Press, 1954.

Gambrell, Herbert. *Anson Jones, The Last President of Texas.* Austin: University of Texas Press, 1964.

Gantt, Fred. *The Chief Executive in Texas, A Study in Gubernatorial Leadership.* Austin: University of Texas Press, 1964.

Graham, Philip. *The Life and Poems of Mirabeau B. Lamar.* Chapel Hill: University of
    North Carolina Press, 1938.
Gunther, John. *Inside U.S.A.* New York: Harper, 1951.
Holland, G. A. and Roberts, Violet M. *The Double Log Cabin, History of Parker County.*
    Weatherford, Texas: Herald Publishing, 1937.
Jackson, Mrs. Pearl. *Texas Governors Wives.* Austin: E. L. Steck, 1915.
James, Marquis. *The Raven.* Indianapolis: Bobbs-Merrill, 1929.
Johnson, Allen, ed., *Dictionary of American Biography,* Vol. I. New York: Scribner's,
    1964.
Johnson, Frank W. *A History of Texas and Texans.* Eugene Barker, ed. Chicago:
    American Historical Society, 1914.
Kennedy, John. *Profiles in Courage.* New York: Harper, 1956.
Kinch, Sam and Long, Stuart. *Allan Shivers: The Pied Piper of Texas Politics.* Austin:
    Shoal Creek, 1973.
Kittrell, N. G. *Governors Who Have Been and Other Public Men.* Houston: Dealy-Adey-
    Elgin Co., 1921.
Lester, Paul. *The Great Galveston Disaster.* Galveston: J. Singer Book Co., 1900.
Lubbock, Francis. *Six Decades in Texas.* Austin: Pemberton Press, 1968.
Lynch, James D. *The Bench and Bar of Texas.* By the author, 1885.
Madden, James William. *Charles Allen Culberson, His Life, Character and Public
    Services.* Austin: Gammel's Book Store, 1929.
McKay, S. S. *Texas Politics, 1906-1944.* Lubbock: Texas Tech Press, 1952.
McKay, S. S. *W. Lee O'Daniel and Texas Politics, 1938-1942.* Lubbock: Texas Tech
    Press, 1944.
Mooney, Booth. *Mister Texas, The Story of Coke Stevenson.* Dallas: Texas Printing
    House, 1947.
Nalle, Ouida Ferguson. *The Fergusons of Texas or "Two Governors for the Price of
    One."* San Antonio: Naylor, 1946.
Neff, Pat M. *The Battles of Peace, an Autobiography.* Fort Worth: Pioneer, 1925.
Neighbours, Kenneth. *Robert Simpson Neighbors and the Texas Frontier, 1836-1859.*
    Waco: Texian Press, 1975.
Ramsdell, Charles. *Reconstruction in Texas.* Austin: University of Texas Press, 1910.
Richardson, T. C. *East Texas, Its History and Its Makers.* New York: Lewis Historical
    Publishing Co., 1940.
Smith, Arthur. *Mr. House of Texas.* New York: Funk and Wagnalls Co., 1940.
Smith, Ashbel. *Reminiscences of the Texas Republic.* Austin: The Pemberton Press,
    1967.
Taylor, T. U. *Fifty Years on Forty Acres.* Austin: Alec Book Co., 1938.
Townsend, Charles R. *San Antonio Rose.* Urbana: University of Illinois Press, 1976.
Webb, Walter Prescott, ed., *The Handbook of Texas.* Austin: The Texas State
    Historical Association, 1952.
Winchester, Robert Glenn. *James Pinckney Henderson, Texas' First Governor.* San
    Antonio: Naylor, 1971.
Wharton, Clarence, ed., *Texas Under Many Flags.* Chicago: The American Historical
    Society, Inc., 1930.
Wooton, Dudley, ed., *Comprehensive History of Texas.* Dallas: William G. Scarff, 1898.
Wyatt, Fredeorica and Hooper, Shelton. *Coke R. Stevenson, A Texas Legend.* Junction:
    Shelton Press, 1976.

Magazines and Journals

Connally, John B. "Why Kennedy Went to Texas." *Life*, (March 24, 1967).

German, S. H. "Governor George Thomas Wood." *Southwestern Historical Quarterly*, XX (1916).

Smith, Henry. "Reminiscences of Henry Smith." *Texas State Historical Association Quarterly*, XIV (July, 1910).

Smith, W. Roy. "The Quarrel Between Governor Smith and the Council of the Provisional Government of the Republic." *Texas State Historical Association Quarterly*, V (April, 1902).

Steen, Ralph W. "Analysis of the Work of the General Council of Texas, 1835-1836." *Southwestern Historical Quarterly*, XL (April, 1937).

Vincent, Louella. "Governor George Thomas Wood." *Southwestern Historical Quarterly*, XX (1916).

Newspapers and Pamphlets

Dallas News, July 14, 1934.

Moore, Walter B. *Governors of Texas*. Dallas: Morning News, 1964.

Texas Parade, January, 1973.

Unpublished Manuscripts

Adkins, John Robert. "The Public Career of Andrew Jackson Hamilton." M. A. thesis, University of Texas at Austin, 1947.

Barksdale, Mary Louise Wimberly. "The Gubernatorial Administration of James Stephen Hogg." M. A. thesis, University of Texas at Austin, 1932.

Flusche, Raymond Paul. "Francis Richard Lubbock." M. A. thesis, Texas Tech University, 1947.

Holbert, Ruby Crawford. "The Public Career of James Webb Throckmorton." M. A. thesis, University of Texas at Austin, 1932.

Huckaby, George Portal. "Oscar Branch Colquitt: A Political Biography." Ph. D. dissertation, University of Texas at Austin, 1946.

Kennedy, Maude. "Sam Houston and Secession." M. A. thesis, Southern Methodist University, 1930.

Key, Norvell. "The Texas Senatorial Election of 1942." M. A. thesis, Texas Tech University, 1943.

Landrum, Cyrus A. "The Texas Gubernatorial Campaign of 1945." M. A. thesis, Texas Tech University, 1948.

Manning, George N. "Public Services of James V. Allred." M. A. thesis, Texas Tech University, 1950.

Martin, Ruby Lee. "The Administration of Governor S. W. T. Lanham, 1903-1907." M. A. thesis, University of Texas at Austin, 1937.

Martindale, Robert. "James V. Allred, The Centennial Governor of Texas." M. A. thesis, University of Texas at Austin, 1957.

McDonald, Mattie. "Sam Houston's Texas Administrations, 1836-1838, 1841-1844." M. A. thesis, University of Oklahoma, 1942.

Miller, Benjamin. "Elisha Marshall Pease, A Biography." M. A. thesis, University of Texas at Austin, 1927.

Mills, Warner E. "The Public Career of a Texas Conservative: A Biography of Ross Shaw Sterling." Ph. D. dissertation, John Hopkins University, 1956.

Moore, Louise M. "Pat M. Neff and his Achievements." M. A. thesis, Texas A and I University, 1941.

Myers, Ila Mae. "The Relations of Governor Pendleton Murrah, of Texas, with the Confederate Military Authorities." M. A. thesis, University of Texas at Austin, 1929.

Nickels, Lenora. "The Public Services of Dan Moody." M. A. thesis, Texas Tech University, 1948.

Norton, Frank Edgar. "The Major Administrative Policies of Oran Milo Roberts, with an Introduction to his Life." M. A. thesis, University of Texas at Austin, 1925.

Nunn, William Curtis. "A Study of the State Police During the E. J. Davis Administration." M. A. thesis, University of Texas at Austin, 1931.

Nunn, William Curtis. "Texas During the Administration of E. J. Davis." Ph. D. dissertation, University of Texas at Austin, 1938.

Parr, Ottis. "The Public Services of Pat M. Neff." M. A. thesis, Texas Tech University, 1951.

Partin, James W., Jr. "The Texas Senatorial Election of 1941." M. A. thesis, Texas Tech University, 1941.

Rhoades, Lida. "The Texas Gubernatorial Election of 1912." M. A. thesis, Texas Tech University, 1948.

Rodney, Imogene Burleson. "Early Political Career of Anson Jones." M. A. thesis, University of Texas at Austin, 1939.

St. Clair, Grady Stafford. "The Hogg-Clark Campaign." M. A. thesis, University of Texas at Austin, 1927.

Sims, Arbriel. "The Texas Gubernatorial Campaign of 1940." M. A. thesis, Texas Tech University, 1940.

Sloan, Sallie Everett. "The Presidential Administration of David G. Burnet, March 17-October 22, 1936, with a Sketch of His Career." M. A. thesis, University of Texas at Austin, 1918.

Smith, Alice Darby. "Anson Jones and the Annexation of Texas." M. A. thesis, Southern Methodist University, 1928.

Smith, Maggie Ruhamuh. "The Administration of Governor John Ireland, 1883-1887." M. A. thesis, University of Texas at Austin, 1934.

Smith, Ralph. "The Life of Alexander Horton." M. A. thesis, University of Texas at Austin, 1936.

Steen, Ralph W. "The Political Career of James E. Ferguson, 1914-1917." M. A. thesis, University of Texas at Austin, 1929.

Tenney, James. "The Public Services of Joseph Draper Sayers." M. A. thesis, University of Texas at Austin, 1933.

Wagner, Robert Lancaster. "The Gubernatorial Career of Charles Allen Culberson." M. A. thesis, University of Texas at Austin, 1954.

Webb, Doris. "The Analysis of the Governor's Race of the Democratic Primaries of Texas in 1934." M. A. thesis, Texas Tech University, 1935.

Webb, Juanita Oliver. "The Administration of Governor L. S. Ross, 1887-1891." M. A. thesis, University of Texas at Austin, 1935.

Whiteside, Myrtle. "The Administration of L. S. Ross." M. A. thesis, University of Texas at Austin, 1938.

Wilson, George Permelia. "John Henninger Reagan and the Texas Constitution of 1876." M. A. thesis, Texas Tech University, 1937.

Wooster, Ralph Ancil. "A Historical Study of the Second Presidential Administration of Sam Houston." M. A. thesis, University of Houston, 1950.

Maps

Coursey, Clark. *Courthouses of Texas*. Brownwood: Banner Printing Co., 1962.

Notes

Henry Smith was. . .Daniell, 1916; Smith, W. R.; Johnson, F. W.; Smith, H.

David G. Burnet lived. . .DeShields; Sloan; Clarke; Johnson, F. W.; DeCordova.

Sam Houston established. . .Day; Clarke; James; Smith, Ashbel; McDonald.

Mirabeau Buonaparte Lamar dreamed. . .DeShields; Lubbock; Graham.

Anson Jones was. . .James; Gambrell; Smith, Alice; Rodney.

Henderson led. . .DeCordova; *Biographical Directory of the American Congress*; Smith, R.; Winchester; Lubbock; Daniell, 1916.

George T. Wood was. . .German; Vincent; Friend; Lubbock.

Peter Bell had. . .Johnson, F. W.; Lubbock; Brown, J. H.; Kittrell; Neighbours; *Biographical Directory of the American Congress*; Johnson, Allen; Dixon.

"Smoky" Henderson was. . .DeShields; *Biographical Directory of the Texas Conventions and Congresses*.

E. M. Pease knew. . .Miller; Lubbock.

Hardin Runnels defeated. . .Lubbock; DeShields; Kittrell; *Biographical Directory of the Texas Conventions and Congress*.

The Texans made. . .Lubbock; Friend; Kennedy, M.

Clark's father was. . .*Biographical Directory of the Texas Conventions and Congresses*; Friend; Lubbock; Kennedy, J.

Francis Lubbock met. . .Lubbock; Flusche.

Confederate Texas collapsed. . .Daniell, 1892; Myers; Kittrell.

Abraham Lincoln made. . .Adkins; Nunn; Daniell, 1892; Lynch, J.

James Throckmorton voted. . .Elliott; Holbert.

A Yankee made. . .Miller; DeShields; Lubbock.

E. J. Davis was. . .Nunn, 1931, 1938; Ramsdell.

Richard Coke threw. . .Brown, J. H.; Lubbock; Nunn; Wilson.

Richard Hubbard weighed. . .Kittrell; Wooten.

Roberts was. . .Taylor; Kittrell; Norton; Wooten.

Ireland was. . .Smith, M.; Lubbock; Wooten.

Sul Ross was. . .Webb; Whiteside; DeShields; Lubbock.

Jim Hogg was. . .Fitzgerald; St. Clair; Smith, Arthur; Barksdale.

Culberson spent. . .Madden; Wagner.

Sayers was. . .Lester; Tenney.

Lanham prosecuted. . .Martin; Holland.

Joe Bailey proclaimed. . .McKay, 1952; Kittrell; Cotner; Adams; Wharton.

O. B. Colquitt fought. . .Rhoades; Huckaby.

Jim Ferguson was. . .Steen, 1929; McKay, 1952.

Will Hobby was. . .Clark, J.; McKay, 1952.

Pat Neff was. . .Parr; Moore; Neff.

Mrs. Ferguson was. . .Nalle; McKay, 1952; Acheson; Gunther.

Dan Moody was. . .Nickels; Acheson.

Ross Sterling was. . .McKay, 1952; Mills; Warner; Clark, J.; Richardson, T. C.

Jimmy Allred hosted. . .Manning; McKay, 1952; Martindale; Webb; *Dallas News*.

W. Lee O'Daniel changed. . .Townsend; McKay, 1944; Sims; Partin; Key.

"Calculating Coke" was. . .Mooney; Wyatt; McKay, 1952.

Beauford Jester died. . .Landrum; Wharton.

Allan Shivers served. . .Kinch.
Price Daniel ran. . .Bartley; *Current Biography*; Banks.
John Connally was. . .Banks; Crawford; Connally.
Preston Smith grew. . .Conn.
Dolph Briscoe won. . .Banks; *Texas Parade*.
Bill Clements was . . . "Bill Clements," *Dallas News*, August 23, 1984.
Mark White provoked . . . *Time* October 11, 1982. *Newsweek* October 4, 1982;
  Newsweek, February 22, 1982; *D* April 1985.

Index